# CONRAD CELTIS
## THE GERMAN ARCH-HUMANIST

# CONRAD CELTIS

## The German Arch-Humanist

WITHDRAWN

Lewis W. Spitz

CAMBRIDGE - HARVARD UNIVERSITY PRESS - 1957

*Distributed in Great Britain by
Oxford University Press, London*

LIBRARY OF CONGRESS CATALOG CARD NUMBER 57-9080
PRINTED IN THE UNITED STATES OF AMERICA

*TO*
EDNA MARIE

# Foreword

THE *interpretation* of the northern Renaissance has been subject to the same changing emphases as that of the Italian Renaissance. Indeed, it has had to consider many factors foreign to the Italian situation which has rendered the problem equally as subtle and complex. Nevertheless, it is not necessary to read from the difficulties a lesson in relativity, for much progress has been made in the understanding of the northern phase of this period of European intellectual history. Significantly, since the publication of Joachimsen's clear and positive definition of humanism describing it as an intellectual movement, primarily literary and philological, which was rooted in the love of and desire for the rebirth of classical antiquity, discussion of the conceptual problems has greatly subsided and there has been a more general agreement that at last a satisfactory working definition has been formulated. Further progress in our understanding of German humanism must be sought in a twofold direction. First of all there is a need for the additional publication of source materials, especially editions of the humanist letters. Secondly, there is a need for discerning biographical studies, particularly since many of the deeply rooted errors as to the nature of northern humanism are imbedded above all in the biographical monographs insofar as they stand uncritically under the influence of Burckhardtian ideas.

A man worthy of special attention because of his central position as a self-conscious and self-styled leader of the German humanists is Conrad Celtis. Even before the appearance of Jakob Burckhardt's great essay on the Renaissance, D. F. Strauss had christened Celtis the German "arch-humanist" (1858). The name has tagged him ever since. Celtis was the first German poet laureate, the inspiration behind many literary and historical projects, a would-be reformer of university education, a playwright, poet, patriot, philosopher of sorts, and a leader of humanist sodalities. Moreover, his candid and often naïve self-revelations make him a particularly accessible and rewarding personality for examination. His life spanned the most important years in the development of the humanist movement in Germany and fell just short of the advent of the Reformation. The student of a pioneer such as Agricola and the teacher of a reformer such as Zwingli, he lived from 1459 to 1508 and may well serve as a case study in the northern Renaissance, as German humanism moved toward its climax and dénouement.

More a poet than a scholar, vain, frivolous, erotic, Celtis had as much as any of his countrymen a "Renaissance" personality. Like Hutten, he had a full share of cheerful optimism and youthful energy. The sixteenth was a bold, vehement, and lusty century. Somehow Celtis seemed more at home in it than the sensible and moderate Erasmus or the sensitive and reflective Mutian. Celtis was the great propagandist for humanism. "Turn, oh Germans, turn to the more gentle studies!" he cried. He was the inspiration and life of the sodalities which added so much to the humanists' self-consciousness and confidence and helped to put the scholastics further on the defensive. In his spontaneous enthusiasm for classic culture and the freedom of his way of life, Celtis represented the left wing among the German humanists. He was typical, moreover, of two major tendencies in German humanism—the mounting tide of romantic cultural nationalism and the interest in religious en-lightenment—which greatly stirred this troubled generation on the eve of the Reformation. Lytton Strachey described the biographical art as "the most delicate and humane of all the branches of the art of writing." It is my hope that Celtis will here emerge from the shrouds of time and documentary La-tinity with some measure of that vitality which characterized his personality and colorful career. May his story afford the reader some pleasurable moments with a sociable intellectual who was once such very good company.

My debt of gratitude is large indeed for such a small book. First and foremost I wish to thank my good friend Professor Myron P. Gilmore of Harvard University, who read the en-tire manuscript and made many valuable suggestions. I am grateful also to Professor Hans Rupprich, noted Renaissance scholar at the University of Vienna, who read the manuscript, made a number of helpful suggestions, and directed my atten-tion to significant materials in the Wiener Universitätsarchiv and the Österreichische Nationalbibliothek. My gratitude is due to my talented friend Dr. George C. Schoolfield for turn-ing the *Ode to Apollo* at the end of the first chapter into good English verse. A Fulbright Scholarship made it possible for me to consult the primary archival and library research ma-terials in Vienna, Munich, and Heidelberg in addition to the sources available in Harvard's Widener and Houghton Li-braries and the Radcliffe College Library. I am thankful to Count and Countess Paul Esterházy and Countess Helene Esterházy for their friendship and hospitality during my stay in Vienna. I wish particularly to thank the Research Council of the University of Missouri for its very generous subsidy toward the cost of publication; and I wish also to express my gratitude to the Ford Foundation. I gratefully acknowledge the assistance of Mrs. Wilbert Rosin who typed the manu-script.

## FOREWORD

Dr. John Herman Randall, Jr., Dr. M. A. Shaaber, and the executive board of the Renaissance Society of America have kindly permitted me to use as part of Chapter 11 my article on "The Philosophy of Conrad Celtis" which appeared previously in *Studies in the Renaissance*, I (1954).

Lewis W. Spitz

*University of Missouri*
*Columbia, Missouri*

# Contents

# CONRAD CELTIS
### THE GERMAN ARCH-HUMANIST

*Utinam talis essem qualem illi me predicant*
*Malo tamen vel falso laudari quam vere vituperari.*
—Conradus Celtis de se ipso

# The First Poet Laureate

CONRAD CELTIS was born three hours after midnight on February 1, 1459, less than a month and a half before Maximilian, that Habsburg prince to whose fortunes and favor his life was to be so closely bound. He was destined to become a poet crowned with laurel, for, if we are to believe him, at the moment of his birth Phoebus sang: "Be born of Phoebus, whoever you will be. You yourself shall play my cither with ivory lyre." The road to such preëminence was, however, difficult and rather more earthy than ethereal.

The son of a peasant, Celtis was born in Wipfeld, a little village in the heart of Germany. His father, Hans Bickel, was an industrious vintager who worked Conrad hard and insisted that he succeed him on the land. In later life Celtis tended especially in adverse times to idealize his life at home working among the vines of Bacchus where sweet hills echoed his joyous song, but at the time the work was galling and he despised it heartily.

Another ideal inspired him—the career of that restless and nervous Gregor Heimburg, doctor of laws, relentless and aggressive opponent of Pope Pius II. Celtis presumably was related to him on his mother's side. However remote the connection, it was a point of pride with Celtis and must have contributed both to his inner resources and to his discontent. An older brother, possibly a monk at the nearby monastery of

Hindenfeld, taught him his first Latin and may have awakened his first interest in literary studies and music.

Since his father remained adamant, the only solution lay in flight. He boarded a raft carrying lumber down the Main to the lower Rhine. He did not flee from a monastery as Hutten did at seventeen, nor to a monastery as Luther did at twenty-two, but merely ran away to school, a revolt which involved neither trauma nor serious regret. He was eighteen when, on October 9, 1477, he registered as a scholar at the University of Cologne.

The University was intellectually a victim of inertia. In an exaggerated ode to Wilhelm Mommerloch, presumably a fellow student of his at the University, Celtis expressed his reaction to his education at Cologne.[1] He resented the scholastic dialectic and fraudulent syllogisms. Here he did learn from Albert and Thomas the sacred books of wisdom and about physical things. But there was no opportunity to study Latin grammar or polished rhetoric nor the secrets of numerology, of astronomy, or Ptolemaic geography. The classics, as Ovid and Cicero, were ridiculed and held suspect. Among all his friends there, Mommerloch alone was interested in these higher matters.

Celtis conformed sufficiently to receive the baccalaureate on December 1, 1479, as "Conradus Bickel de Sweinfordia pauper." Perhaps during these years Celtis as a *pauper* supported himself by personal service to some of the *nobiles*, a recognized class of prosperous students. Or perhaps one can suppose that he was cared for by the Brethren of the Common Life who had a house there and considered it one of their most important duties to care for poor but gifted students. He probably spent at least some time between 1479 and 1484 in further study. During these years also he must have traveled in the region of the lower Rhine, for, until their temporary expulsion for misconduct in 1482, there were many students from Holland, Zeeland, and Frisia at Cologne whom he might have visited.

Drawn by the fame of Rudolf Agricola and Johannes von Dalberg, Celtis moved on to Heidelberg University where he matriculated on December 13, 1484, and on April 11, 1485, he was accepted by the arts faculty as a bachelor of arts from Cologne. Among the German universities, Heidelberg was a relatively early friend of humanism. The reign of Elector Philipp, who in 1476 inherited the rule over the Palatinate from his warlike uncle, Frederick the Victorious, was most propitious to the cause of learning. Politically fortunate, he was allowed a long period of peace for the development of cultural life. During his reign the University prospered.

The traditional picture of the sharp opposition of the University to the new learning, of a severe conflict between the scholastic dominated faculty of arts and the new intellectuals of Philipp's court, as well as the extreme hostility of the two scholastic *viae* to each other within the University, must be reconsidered.[2] Rather, so long as humanism meant primarily a new form of rhetorical expression and the continuation and gradual acceleration of interest in antiquity there was little room for conflict with scholasticism. Celtis himself spanned the distance, such as it was, between the University and the court. He hewed to the line and received first the licentiate of liberal arts in the realist *via* on October 10, 1485, and, ten days later, his master's degree. He belonged at the same time to the circle of the humanist chancellor of Elector Philipp, the Bishop of Worms, Johannes von Dalberg.

To this circle, and also dividing his attention between the court at Worms and Heidelberg belonged Rudolf Agricola, the man of whom Erasmus said, "He could have been the first man in Italy had he not preferred Germany." Agricola may be considered the first German humanist in the full sense of the word. Author, musician, artist, and scholar of versatile learning, he was a master as an elegant courtier. And yet there was much in Agricola which did not stem from the spirit of Italian humanism. He kept his earnest piety rooted in his boyhood days in Groningen. He had studied the arts at northern universities before going to Italy and reflected in many areas of thought a conservative outlook. Agricola left little behind in writing, but the real key to his importance lies in his direct personal influence.

What was it that attracted Celtis to him? In an ode published before his *Ars versificandi* in 1486, a year after Agricola's death, Celtis praised him as the man who introduced him to Italian learning before he himself had the opportunity of wandering through Latium or in the hills of Euboea. It was his humanist learning, his music, and his fame, rather than his piety, which impressed young Celtis. At least so it seemed to him in retrospect. That Celtis learned much Greek and Hebrew from Agricola is improbable for he was with him in Heidelberg for less than half a year. In May 1485, Agricola went with Dalberg to Italy and returned a very sick man in September. On October 27 he died. When he died, Celtis left Heidelberg.

This time, however, Celtis traveled, not as a mere student, but as a teacher. At the end of 1485 or the beginning of 1486 he arrived at "many towered Erfurt" toward the end of the winter semester. Succeeding a mediocre poet, Johannes Riedner, the most recent of a number of wandering poets at Erfurt such as Peter Luder and Samuel Karoch, Celtis supported himself rather well by teaching poetry and rhetoric. Without doubt his most important pupil was Mutianus Rufus, later to become the head of the Erfurt humanists.

Restless, Celtis moved on, possibly to Rostock first, then to Leipzig. With his arrival in Leipzig, he gives evidence of an increasing self-consciousness and determination to make his mark. He now added the graecized Protucius, like Erasmus' Desiderius, as a third name in the manner of the Roman poets. He took up his very rewarding teaching with enthusiasm, lecturing on Ciceronian rhetoric, the verse of Horace, and the construction of antique meter. He taught some Greek, though it was precious little, for that was all he knew. Here, too, he followed the footsteps of the "Wandervögel" of early humanism—Luder, Politian, and Karoch. He was a popular teacher and that very summer he resolved to publish a study of poetry drawn, we may suppose, largely from his lectures, the *Ars versificandi et carminum*. It was one of the first independent studies of poetry in German literature and the first extant work of Celtis.[3]

The *Ars versificandi* was formally in the medieval tradition and comparable to the medieval poesy of a Galfred of Vinosalvo. The leonine mnemonic verses in the first part are in the medieval tradition. Indeed, without naming Alexander Gallus, so despised by the progressive humanists, he used him directly. The humanists maintained the medieval custom of presenting purely grammatical portions in verse form. But with all its conformity to the standard pattern, some of Celtis' new verve emerges, as in his definition of the poet.

For the true poet's task is to present in picturesque and beautiful garment of speech and of song the customs, affairs, happenings, localities, peoples, lands, rivers, the course of the stars, the true essence of all things, and what moves the heart of man.

During the winter semester Celtis began a new project designed as an aid to teaching, an edition of Seneca's tragedies. It was to be modeled after the *Editio princeps* which appeared at Ferrara in 1484. He began with the publication of the *Hercules furens*, in February 1487, followed by the second tragedy, *Thyestes*, a little later.[4] Celtis never published more than these two for, contrary to his original plans, he left Leipzig soon thereafter.

This preoccupation with Seneca, who had interested Agricola already and whose dramas were often republished thereafter, frequently by university professors, demonstrates an interest in the dramatic form explored already by Mussato and his circle. As Celtis observed in the *Ars*, Seneca is a master of brilliant balanced diction. Basically, however, it was another more medieval interest which attracted Celtis to Seneca whose dramas had after all been rediscovered and appreciated already around 1300. This is the factor which Celtis chose to emphasize in his prefaces addressed to the very religious Prince Magnus von Anhalt, ruler of Zerbst, at any rate. The dramas should serve above all to instruct the princes, for they are the tutors of the *Respublica Christiana* among whom none can contend with the Prince of Anhalt in virtue, sacred morals, and the splendor of letters. Both the pragmatic purpose of teaching morality and the conception of tragedy reveal a traditional medieval conception of the drama.

Celtis was not long in receiving his reward. Frederick the Wise of Saxony, to whom he had dedicated the *Ars versificandi* in which he subtly hinted at the laurel, urged the Holy Roman Emperor, Frederick III, to crown him poet laureate. The petition for the laurel and the elegiac poem which accompanied it were well received. Celtis was following Petrarch who had been crowned in Rome and by Charles IV in Pisa, the first crowning by an Emperor of the German nation. In vain Boccaccio mocked the "Bohemian emperor" and the "Pisan laurel," the crown remained a coveted prize. Frederick himself in 1442 had adorned Aeneas Silvius with laurel in Frankfort, the first crowning on German soil, an event immortalized by Bernardino Pinturicchio in the cathedral library of Siena. Frederick was so lavish with titles that Giovanni Mario Filelfo was quite right in being amused at the many knights, counts Palatine, and imperial poets upon whom he bestowed titles.[5]

Frederick's fortunes were at their usual low ebb. He had been driven from Vienna by the Hungarian king, Matthias Corvinus, and spent most of the year 1487 in Nuremberg. He called a Reichstag for March 18 and among the princes who arrived during the next month or so were Philipp of the Palatinate and the dukes of Saxony, Johann and Frederick the Elector, who arrived with Celtis no doubt in the entourage on March 28. It was a futile Reichstag, replete with pomp and gestures reminiscent of the Burgundian crusade rallies, and it achieved nothing against either Hungarians or Turks. Celtis called in vain for action against the Turks.[6] On April 18 more festivities and a tournament in honor of the emperor were held. Then on the citadel, perhaps in the so-called hanging gardens the poet's crowning took place. The emperor, who himself spoke a halting Latin, embraced the kneeling poet, kissed his cheek, crowned him with a laurel wreath and placed on his head the doctor's hood. In the diploma of award, Frederick declared that he, as his predecessors, Octavian, Tiberius, Julius Caesar, and many other emperors, considered the poet worthy of highest honors. As among the Greeks so also in his court learning and poetry were cherished. Celtis had given a taste of poetic learning and had recited many elegant verses before him. Therefore he invested Celtis, as he had done others, with the honors, privileges, liberties, favors, and prerogatives of the poet laureate.[7] For all the ceremony, the crowning did not make much of an impression. Most of the Chronicles refer to it in just a few words and even Celtis' close friend Hartmann Schedel in his *Nuremberg Chronicle* merely commented that "Frederick III among other praiseworthy deeds also ornamented Conrad Celtis, an exceptionally learned man, on the citadel with the laurel wreath of Apollo." That is all.

Celtis at least was deeply moved.

> *One born under wretched roof,*
> *Son of a father digging a hard field,*
> *Is raised by fate*
> *And seizes highest honors.*[8]

How important it was that he should be a poet and sing his songs throughout the fatherland! He noted the position of the stars at the exact instant in which the laurel touched his temples, an augury of great things to come. Celtis responded with a *Proseuticum ad diuum Fridericum tercium*, a collection of poems dedicated in a letter dated April 25 to Duke George of Saxony. It became a model for later gestures of thanks by other poets, as Jakob Locher and Heinrich Bebel.

Celtis remained in Nuremberg for only a brief time after the crowning. On May 9 he sent his *Proseuticum* together with a poem of ten distichs to Hieronymus Münzer, his host, a Nuremberg doctor. At the end he sent his greetings to Johannes von Dalberg, who had accompanied Count Philipp to the Reichstag, which may indicate that Celtis was no longer in Nuremberg himself.[9]

It is probable that Celtis returned to Leipzig, but for a brief time only. In his rise to highest honors he did not fail to offend and antagonize. There is no special evidence of hostility between him and the professors of scholastic philosophy. Rather, he fell out with his fellow humanists. The physician of Frederick the Wise, Martin Pollich of Mellerstadt, had drawn the attention of the prince to Celtis. The Bohemian humanist Bohuslaus Lobkowitz von Hassenstein had also exchanged letters with Celtis and befriended him. Suddenly the friendship came to an end. Bohuslaus in two letters to Mellerstadt referring almost certainly to Celtis tells us all that we know about his exit from Leipzig.[10] In the first letter he charges that Conrad in his great desire to seek authority and gain glory with his own students plagiarized and published under his own name not only his poems, but those of Gregorius Tyfernius and even of Virgil and Homer. In the second letter Bohuslaus expresses satisfaction that Mellerstadt, shocked, had broken off his friendship with Conrad, avoiding him entirely and that Conrad had left for Gaul. Moreover, wrote Bohuslaus, Leipzig would not suffer a loss, for Priamus, superior to Conrad in all fields of teaching, a man of genius and erudition, would succeed him. Priamus Capotius of Sicily did, indeed, succeed Celtis at Leipzig. It was hostility to Celtis, not to the *studia humanitatis* which drove Celtis from Leipzig. It became a *cause célèbre* with the humanists anyway and as late as 1511 Aesticampianus, a student of Celtis and the teacher of Hutten, attacked Leipzig for expelling Celtis in hostility.[11]

In those early uncertain days Celtis did, to be sure, choose the road to quick fame—and infamy. In Rome, Jacob Questenberg saw on a parchment in the Church of Maria Nuova a hymn of Gregorius Tyfernius to the Virgin Mary and apparently he acquired at the same time a print of a poem by Celtis to the Virgin exactly the same, but without Tyfernius' name. Enraged he wrote an invective against "The Ass in the Stolen Lion's Head."[12] The poet laureate must have had some bitter moments, when in 1500, over a decade later, his student Vincentius Longinus traveling in Italy sent Questenberg's poem to his patron and friend, the head of the Rhenish humanists, Johannes von Dalberg. Celtis may also have entertained the idea of circulating his own composition under Ovid's name as the long lost books of the *Fasti*, but may have dropped the plan because of the suspicions of the publisher Aldus Manutius.[13] It is possible that he himself may have been deceived in thinking he possessed a copy. At least Celtis did not compound the felony with an oath like his dear friend Trithemius, notorious as a forger, who pronounced solemnly in the preface to his

*Hirschauer Chronicle* that he as a Christian and a member of an Order was incapable of a lie.

Celtis may have gone first to France, though it seems unlikely. It was rather sunny Italy that beckoned him, that land of classic splendor, that land of brilliance so different from the barbarous North. Celtis was twenty-eight when, in the summer of 1487, he crossed the Alps for the first and only time. He went not just to admire the land of ancient Rome, but to bring its muses like the Imperium northward. In his "Ode to Apollo"[14] he expressed this thought beautifully and thereby laid down the program for the northern humanists:

## Ode to Apollo

> *Phoebus, who the sweet-noted lyre constructed,*
> *Leave fair Helicon and depart your Pindus,*
> *And by pleasant song designated, hasten*
>      *To these our borders.*
>
> *You perceive how joyous the Muses gather,*
> *Sweetly singing under a frozen heaven;*
> *Come yourself, and with your melodious harp-strings,*
>      *Gaze on these wastelands.*
>
> *So must he, whom sometime a rude or rustic*
> *Parent fostered, barbarous, all unknowing*
> *Latium's splendors, choose you now as his teacher*
>      *At writing verses.*
>
> *Just as Orpheus sang to the old Pelasgians,*
> *Orpheus, whom swift stags, beasts of savage custom,*
> *Whom the lofty trees of the forest followed,*
>      *Charmed by his plectrum.*
>
> *Swift and joyous, once you forswore, and gladly,*
> *Greece for Latium, passing the mighty ocean;*
> *There you wished your delectable arts to broadcast,*
>      *Leading the Muses.*
>
> *Thus it is our prayer you may wish to visit*
> *Our abode, as once those Italian reaches.*
> *May wild tongue take flight, and may all of darkness*
>      *Come to destruction.*

2

# The Wandering Humanist

CELTIS was a wanderer. Throughout his life, driven by a restless dynamism, he was impelled onward even when comfort and security were to be found at hand. The student wandering was, of course, an old tradition and by his day the paths southward to Italian schools were much traveled. But the novel element in the character of Celtis, not to be found in like measure in more sober personalities, was his intense yet undisciplined will to learn, his eagerness to see and to experience the new, and his self-consciousness as to the purpose and importance of his travels. He never tired of referring particularly his geographical knowledge to his "ten years of wandering," by which he most likely meant the years from his poet's crowning to his permanent residence in Vienna, 1487-1497. Always his travels had a broad and at times nebulous objective. Dürer might journey to Florence and Rome to learn from the work of Michelangelo, Vesalius might go to Padua to study anatomy and Copernicus to Ferrara, Celtis went to each of these and elsewhere. But he stayed nowhere for long.

Following the busy trade route southward in the summer of 1487 Celtis arrived at the queen city of the Adriatic—Venice. Here he studied with Marcus Sabellicus, historian, philologist, and librarian at St. Mark's. Celtis later charged him with boast-

• • 11 •

ing he had equaled the Romans, disparaging the titles of German princes, and calling them barbarians. It is understandable that he should have offended the newly crowned, sensitive poet laureate of the North. In nearby Padua taught John Calphurnius of Brescia, professor of grammar and rhetoric and a prominent Terence scholar, and L. Camers or Creticus, as he was called because of his seven years of study in Crete, professor of Greek at the University. These were the men who attracted Celtis to Padua. It is not likely that Celtis was drawn from his favorite rhetorical studies to averroism, the leading philosophy since the first half of the fourteenth century. Perhaps it was high prices in Padua which drove Celtis, with his rapidly dwindling savings, onward. Whatever the reason, he proceeded to Ferrara and again took up the study of Latin and Greek literature, this time with the Veronese Baptista Guarinus. At Bologna, Celtis must have found an atmosphere more congenial to a northerner, but less congenial to a poet. Philippus Beroaldus with whom he studied was a spirited much traveled man, very much closer to the scholastic mentality than most of his fellow humanists and very friendly to German students. He was an editor and translator, but in no sense creative.

In Florence, Ficino was working on the *De triplici vita*, that "diatetic of the saturnine man," to be published a year or so later. He was already well known for his Platonic studies, above all for his Plato translation of 1483/1484. Small wonder that Celtis was drawn to Florence where he learned to know Ficino personally. Here he encountered a philosophy attuned to his poetic spirit. He did not subject himself to disciplined study and was not inclined to follow a technical philosophical argument, but the idea of novelty, a different approach to formal intellectual problems, a new enthusiasm captivated him. On to Rome!

The contrast in Rome between the ancient ruins and the

new city, between the grandeur of former days and the modern racketeering reality was even greater near the end of the fifteenth century than it is at present. How little remained of the old fame and brilliance, of the power of world empire. Aeneas Silvius penned: "It delights me, Rome, to see your ruins, from whose fall ancient glories are displayed." He determined to preserve what remained and to rebuild. Celtis' reaction was one neither of pity nor of inspiration. He did not seem to feel its art and beauty. Rather, from the many epigrams on Rome, emerge feelings of antipathy and mocking. Only one contains a note of regret.

### On entering Rome

*What is left, O Rome, except the fame of your ruin,*
*Of so many consuls and caesars together?*
*Consuming time thus devours all things and nothing*
*Stands perpetual in the world. Virtue and books*
*    alone remain.*[1]

The Rome of Innocent VIII was indeed something short of inspirational. John Baptista Cibò was himself mocked as the father of his country because he readily acknowledged his prodigious number of offspring. The struggles of the Colonna and Orsini kept the city in constant turmoil, and the war with Naples kept the city in constant danger. The bands of brigands outside the city and the independence of the intriguing cardinals within produced a virtual anarchy. What a contrast to the days of the Republic. Rome was besieged with vulturous courtesans. The city which once sold bodies now sold souls. Whatever wealth Germany possessed in farthest lands has been exhausted and taken to Latin citadels, so that impious Rome might satisfy its luxuries. The monies that should be used for soldiers to defend homes are used only for Venus and Bacchus night and day. What rankled Celtis above all was that in his audience with Innocent he was expected to kiss his foot. When

Sulla once had conquered Marius, he stretched out his hands for Rome to kiss. How fortunate to live now in this day and age, when pious Rome kisses the sacred feet![2] What a contrast to his treatment at the hands of his own Caesar:

*Concerning the kiss of the Emperor and of the Pope*

*When you gave the sacred crown, Frederick, my Emperor,*
*You placed bland kisses on our cheeks.*
*But when at Rome I saw the house of Innocent (Nocentis),*
*He commanded me to kiss his foot.*
*I, lying prone, gave kisses, but the lips of Caesar*
*delight me more*
*Than to give kisses to a noxious foot.*[3]

Here we have a theme ringing with the anti-papal fervor of the Reformation. Indeed, Luther attacked the same practice: "The kissing of the pope's feet should cease. It is an unchristian, nay, an antichristian thing for a poor sinful man to let his feet be kissed by one who is a hundred times better than himself. If it is done in honor of his authority, why does not the pope do the same to others in honor of their holiness? Compare the two—Christ and the pope!"[4] Lucas Cranach did two wood carvings, the one showing Christ washing the disciples feet; the other showing the pope extending his toe to be kissed. But Celtis' pique was not moral indignation. It was rather the reaction of a proud and sensitive northerner to his neglect and humiliation at the hands of the Italians. It was more in the manner of Hutten.

The discovery of the body of a Roman girl found by workers in the Via Appia in 1485 provided Celtis with an occasion for an epigram which presents succinctly his anti-Roman spirit. The find caused great excitement, not unlike that produced in the Middle Ages by the discovery of the huge body of Pallas, and it was noised abroad that here was greater beauty than could now be found anywhere. Though Innocent VIII, with little feeling for the cult of the aesthetic or of pagan antiquity, had the body secretly interred, the sarcophagus remained and there was still much talk of it when Celtis was in Rome.

> *Concerning a Girl Found at Rome*
> *A thousand years enclosed within this tomb I lay*
> *Now released from this tomb to you Romans, I say:*
> *I do not now see Roman citizens in the manner of old,*
> *Distinguished for justice and men of piety.*
> *But with sad heart I look upon such great ruins,*
> *Now only a monument to the men of times past.*
> *And if again I shall see you after a hundred years,*
> *Scarcely anything I think will be left of the Roman name.*[5]

At least Celtis gained one positive idea in Rome which was to be of the greatest significance to his future activity. He learned from the Platonic Academy of Pomponius Laetus the value of association for the cause of humanist learning.

Celtis having concentrated, formally at least, on the study of grammar and rhetoric on his Italian trip, was developing an increasing interest in natural science, in mathematics and astronomy. Perhaps he learned of Cracow University from Pomponius, for a former member of his Academy before his expulsion from Rome by Paul II, Callimachus, was teaching there. Suddenly Celtis decided to go to Cracow and hurriedly he left Rome. He returned to Venice and from there, via Trieste, proceeded through Croatia and Hungary to Cracow arriving around Easter in 1489.

Cracow University had been founded twice, once by King Casimir in 1346 and again in 1400 by Jagiello, Grand Duke of Lithuania and King of Poland, who had himself once been a pagan, so closely did the heathenism of the North impinge upon the Quattrocento. The University benefited from an influx of Prague professors during the Hussite rebellion and during the last decades of the century enjoyed a flowering of intellectual activity and a general prosperity which it seldom equalled thereafter. Celtis found it a most congenial place and stayed two years. At the age of thirty he assumed once again the double role of student and teacher, matriculating for the summer semester of 1489.

Celtis had come to learn about the world of nature and the man of leading reputation from whom he could learn was Albert Blar or Brudzewo. He had been a student of Peuerbach, whose book on the planets he edited a few years later, and of Regiomontanus, and later became himself the teacher of Copernicus. These men were far from being great innovators and revolutionaries as sometimes depicted. Brudzewo lectured on Aristotle, arithmetic, and astronomy. In 1490 he received the bachelor of theology degree, became canon of St. Florian, and dedicated himself to the study of scholasticism. Celtis was his student and close personal friend, corresponding with him later and dedicating an ode to him. Celtis, for all his interest in astronomy, did not feel called upon to continue work on the problems left by Regiomontanus. His interest in astronomy, stemmed rather from a romantic poetic enthusiasm; insofar as it had any disciplined aspect at all, it was directed toward that pseudo-science, astrology, which rode a new crest of popularity with the coming of the humanists.

As usual, Celtis managed to provoke the hostility of some of the older professors. It would be an error to interpret this friction as the opposition of the scholastic "sophists" to the new learning, for the leaders of the University were quite tolerant of humanist studies. Celtis maintained himself once more by teaching, not only privately, but giving public lectures on rhetoric, poetry, and the art of letter writing in the Hungarian bursa. In the summer of 1490 he lectured on the Aristotelian *Parvulus philosophiae*, his furthest departure in teaching from his standard *ars humanitatis* fare.[6]

Through his formal teaching and by personal contact Celtis had a lasting influence on some of the students who were to play an important part in the humanist movement of the Northeast. One of those whom Celtis converted to the humanist interest was Laurentius Corvinus, who became in turn the teacher of Heinrich Bebel and of Copernicus at Cracow. It was he who really introduced humanism belatedly to Silesia though he had never left German and Polish soil. Later he played a leading role in the cause of the Reformation in Silesia.[7] The relationship of Celtis to his court friends, fellow professors, and students was at Cracow informal. He seems not to have advanced the idea of an academy or association of humanists such as in later years he actively promoted.

Celtis was a keen, but not a systematic observer. His impressions of Poland are reflected in his poems: the favorable ones in his odes and elegies, the less pleasant concealed in his epigrams. It seems probable that during the summer he spent in Danzig, in 1489 or 1490, he gathered his seafaring yarns about the island of Thule beyond the Orkneys and may himself have ventured out upon the Baltic, perhaps to Rostock and Lübeck or as far as Sweden, certainly not so far as Lapland. His stay in Poland provided other adventures—such as the hazardous hunt for bison, the trip through the salt mines of Wieliczka which he compared with an excursion through Tartarus, and the exploration of the Carpathians.

But Celtis found much to criticize. Poland was after all a cold and barbarous land with few cities. He detested the peasant huts and the wildness of the lower classes—eating horse meat and drinking without restraint. He chided the effeminacy of the upper classes who in the summer needed feather beds for warmth. Small wonder that, as in the land of the Amazons, the women rule the men![8]

It was not only the love of learning and the attraction of the Polish landscape which held Celtis in Cracow. Here he learned to know Hasilina von Rzytonic, the first of his many loves. His loves tended definitely downward in the social scale, but Hasilina at least was connected with a good Polish family. Her husband was an old Polish nobleman living in Cracow who was not entirely unaware of his young wife's philandering. Hasilina's appeal for Celtis had nothing at all in common with the attraction of such ladies as Beatrice or Laura. Celtis had many rivals for her attention and, rejected after a full year's courtship, left Sarmatian lands embittered.

He made good his threat that, if spurned, Phoebus would spread her name throughout all the earth. She it was who became the heroine of the first book of the *Amores* and the subject of many odes. His poems are personal and unveiled and reveal an interest in only the physical possession of the beloved. A decade later Hasilina wrote him an indignant letter, relating the embarrassment caused her by his poems and begging him to suppress them. Still later, his Cracow friends Sommerfeld and Corvinus wrote to him that time had claimed its own, Hasilina was widowed and still remembered Celtis. If he thought of marriage then, it was neither seriously nor for long.

It was late summer in 1491 when Celtis left Poland for his homeland. He was in a cantankerous mood and stirred up enough excitement along the way to prevent a dull trip. His journey took him first to Breslau in Silesia, then through Bohemia and Moravia to Nuremberg. His reaction to Breslau was none too gratifying, but he found Bohemia insufferable. He stayed at the home of Jacobus Argyrius, a professor at the University of Prague. But his hospitality was not sufficient to allay Celtis' dislike for the Bohemians and his ire at their ways. He gave vent to his feelings about their customs and beliefs in a series of caustic epigrams which were publicized prematurely and generated such hatred that he escaped popular vengeance only by precipitous flight. To Celtis, Hus was nothing more than a cooked goose.[9] The Bohemians jested against the Roman pontiff, declaring that, when a Roman official set foot in the land, blossoms failed to bud, women lost fertility, and plagues descended on the land. Bohemia alone among all the nations dared to condemn the Latin laws and drink of the sacred liquid. The Bohemians instituted new ceremonial rites and approved the forbidden laws written by that Britisher Wycliffe.[10]

This animus against the Bohemians was less the indignation of an orthodox Catholic than a kind of cultural nationalism which led him to such abandoned criticism, though the two could not be so clearly distinguished then as now with the clear cut distinction of church and state. The goose had flown noisily among the German swans, but the Italian wolf had grasped her neck, plucked her feathers and burned her in an open fire. The attitude of Celtis, with neither interest nor feeling for dogmatic correctness, was rather one of a plague on both your houses. Small wonder that the people, still filled, as Celtis noted, with the fierce madness of Ziska, were enraged that he had mocked their bishop, their religion, and their fatherland.[11]

In September 1491, Celtis was in Nuremberg once again. He had gained much from his years abroad: a renewed enthusiasm for his old literary studies, a wider range of intellectual interests, especially in nature and the "causes of things," and a new confidence which enabled him to mount the podium and propound reform with the voice of authority. Above all, if we can place credence in one of his poetic flights, it was in Poland that he received a vision of his life's work. For, on a hilltop overlooking the walls and spires of Cracow, Phoebus had appeared to him in a vision and commissioned him to "Rise and let his members seize their ancient vigor so that he might sing of the four corners of his fatherland!"[12] He had broadened his outlook. His goal would be, not only to bring the light of Phoebus northward, but with it to illumine Germany itself.

# Ingolstadt and the Reform of University Education

FOUR YEARS and four months had passed since Celtis had been in Nuremberg for his festive crowning on the Burg towering above the city. Since that elevated moment he had changed much, but it was a change of degree rather than of kind. He was now more sure of himself, more positive, more dogmatic and aggressive. Before the year was out he was already busy preparing an oration in which he would publicly declare his program for the intellectual reform of Germany.

Once more his stay in Nuremberg was brief before he moved on toward his natural habitat, a university town. His circle of friends was growing and included the canon of St. Sebaldus, the art-loving Sebald Schreyer, the doctors Dietrich Ulsenius and Heinrich Euticus the elder, and the wealthy city councilman, Peter Danhauser. His friends made an effort to have him appointed as city poet and head of a new school of poetry; but the majority in the council was not as yet convinced of the necessity for a poet. Discussion continued, but Celtis had meanwhile moved on.

Celtis saw to it that he would be available, should the council make a substantial offer, for, during the last month of the year, he moved to Ingolstadt not far away. Founded in 1472 by Duke George the Rich of Bavaria-Landshut, the University of Ingolstadt was now scarcely twenty years old. Celtis was probably invited to Ingolstadt by the jurist Sixtus Tucher of Nuremberg who had been on the legal faculty since 1487.[1] Celtis needed a friend. It was apparent to him by this time that his luggage with his books, household effects, in fact, almost all his belongings had gone astray en route from Breslau to Nuremberg and he prevailed on Tucher for a loan of eight or ten gulden until he should be able to recoup his loss. Celtis was angry, he stormed and raged against the dishonest Polish wagon driver, and for over a year bombarded all his friends along the route with queries. He was not one to nurse an injury in his bosom.

Celtis once more accepted students for private instruction, possibly receiving a small gift from the University. He was not entered in the matriculation book, however, until February 2, 1492. He decided to remain in Ingolstadt during the coming year, expecting an ordinary lectureship paying at least a hundred Rhenish gulden. He had heard that the professor of poetry and rhetoric was leaving at Easter, and wished to receive his position and his house and open there an *Academia Platonica* for men of learning and good breeding.

There seems to have been some suspicion of Celtis' religious soundness on the part of Johann Permeter von Adorf, one of the leading professors of theology, who, however, when sharply challenged by Celtis, was quick to deny that he had spoken of the poet's views on confession, communion, or other religious questions. On the other hand, he was befriended by another theologian, Georg Zingel, whom he praised for defending the arts against the lawyers. It was rather another man who prevented his permanent appointment and that man was not a theologian, but a poet, Johannes Riedner. He, too, belonged to the genre of traveling poets and had been Celtis' predecessor at Erfurt. He had, since March 4, 1484, been lecturer in poetry and rhetoric at Ingolstadt. As a matter of fact, since Riedner's arrival the study of the humanities had greatly increased in popularity. It was already the fashion to keep a poet at a well-ordered university, and even before the advent of Celtis there had been a rapid increase in the number of humanist-minded students.[2]

Riedner failed to resign at Easter as Celtis had anticipated, infuriating the frustrated poet. The best Celtis could receive was a temporary appointment and that required some strenuous maneuvering. Full of confidence, he began working on his inaugural address around Christmas of 1491, laying down the basis and justification for his lecture program. Except for a two-day visit to nearby Freising, Celtis tended to business, teaching and preparing for his expected appointment. Finally he received, on May 5, 1492, the awaited appointment from Duke George, but only for half a year. In the decretal addressed to Tucher and Baumgartner, the duke suggested forty or forty-two Rhenish gulden as compensation and the university treasurer naturally adopted the lesser alternative. Celtis responded probably with a public recitation and with the publication of the *Panegyris ad duces Bavariae*, possibly published separately in April, though there is no copy extant, and then later published together with the inaugural address and other poems. It is a flattering ingratiating piece singing the praises of the Wittelsbach princes for their generosity and service to learning.

Celtis, quick to advertise his wares, issued a written invitation to the whole University to attend his lectures on Ciceronian rhetoric, the art of letter writing, and mnemonic techniques.[3] As usual, he was direct and pointed, not to say tactless, in driving home some of his pet ideas:

How important and useful for all professors of letters is the knowledge of speaking and writing well and artfully can be learned, as each can see and observe in himself and others, from listening to certain people who speak from the *cathedras* brokenly and crudely against all art and rule of speech like quacking geese or lowing oxen disturbing the ears, pouring forth common, vile, and corrupt words and whatever enters their mouth, pronouncing harshly and barbarously the smooth Latin tongue. And what seems to me to be a particular wonder is that for so many centuries in so many universities in our Germany and with so much scholastic clamor, through which we all wish to be counted learned, no one could be found who could write letters or speeches, poems or histories elegantly and nicely as the Italian race has done in smaller but by far more learned universities. But so it is! That can hardly among the Germans be considered educating the youth, when we bury them with our own ignorance and do not let them learn anything which does not agree with our own sordid learning. What will the future be, since our students always grow up to be the same kind as we their teachers were. Oh, lamentable situation, to neglect so the genius of such noble youths! But forgive me, learned men! For this happens through no fault of yours, but I believe that it is due more to the order of the times and of the fates. Since I find no other cause than that we do not understand the words themselves to which the art of speaking is bound and are not rightly able to order what Cicero has diffusely written in his rhetoric. Considering this defect in our men I have suffered deeply for my Germany, because in so many of our universities there has never been anyone who had expounded Cicero straight forwardly and lucidly. Desiring therefore out of love for the republic of letters to apply a remedy for this disease, we shall reduce to a certain conspicuous and clear order the precepts of speaking and all the vigor, for so I shall speak, of Ciceronian eloquence and these things we have already had printed and we have decided on next Monday at the first hour so to interpret these things and lecture so that all Cicero will now be understood as though he had spoken German rather than Latin. It will be for you a perpetual monument with the most splendid ornament and decoration, whether in preaching to a crowd, or in performing legal transactions, giving counsel, writing letters, orating, or in speaking with whatsoever man you will. Valete.

The work on Ciceronian eloquence which he had already published was his *Epitoma in vtramque Ciceronis rhetoricam* (Ingolstadt, 1492), which was intended to serve as a guide for his lectures during the summer semester now underway. It was dedicated to Maximilian, King of the Romans. Celtis was looking ahead and this was the first of many writings by which he attracted Maximilian's attention. The first part of the *Epitoma* devoted to rhetoric contains the familiar Ciceronian material drawn from the *De inventione rhetorica* and the teachings of the unknown author of *Rhetorica ad Herennium*. In Part Two he suggests rules for easy memorizing based on the notions of the clarity of the original impression and devices for association. In the final part, the *Tractatus de condendis epistolis*, he presents a formal treatise on the art of letter writing. For each major kind of letter Celtis gave a personal example. He illustrated the love letter with a brief but passionate sample asking Hasilina Eugenia for her love, "For what is sweeter, more pleasant, than that we live, love each other, kiss, and jest with each other?" No wonder that there were raised eyebrows in Ingolstadt! Particularly this part of the *Epitoma* became very popular and was reprinted many times thereafter, frequently with Erasmus' *De ratione conscribendi epistolas* and Vives' *De conscribendis epistolis*.

The next two or three months, surprisingly enough, Celtis devoted himself quite diligently to teaching. In the *Panegyric* he had described the benefits of studying the classics, how the youth might learn continence, receive comfort, and be inspired to noble deeds. In addition to Cicero he lectured on Horace and for the first time on the *Cosmography* of Ptolemy, an interest dating doubtless from his Cracow days. Grammar, too, he taught with poetic devices.[4] After a brief midsummer

vacation classes resumed and were to continue without in-
terruption until the end of the summer semester, but not for
Celtis. He delivered his *Inaugural Oration* on August 31, pro-
pounding his ideas on the reform of university education and
then left town a few days later on further adventures.

The *Oratio*, in spite of its loose style and casual organization,
was the product of long deliberation and was the crystalliza-
tion of ideas which he had harbored many years and chose now
to advance with great vigor and vehemence. As early as the
preceding Christmas he had sent a draft of the *Oratio* to
Tucher for correction and in January he submitted it to the
rector of the University, Johannes Kaufmann. Now when at
last he, a lecturer in oratory, was to mount the rostrum to deliver his inaugural address, he could do so with the confidence
that he had an enthusiastic group of student followers and influential friends in the audience. He might need friends.

In a letter written only three weeks later, a friend described
him now at thirty-three as a mature heavy-set man with an ob-
long face, sharpsighted eyes, dark brown bushy hair, white
hands with long fingers and the expression of the countenance
feigned with a slight inclination of the head and with a deep
sounding, hoarse laughter. Such was the appearance and vitality of the rhetorician and orator who now rose before the
University to propound his ideas on educational reform. He
was to devote his life to the realization of the program which
he set forth.[5]

Humanists since Petrarch had substituted the loose style of
the antique, free, suggestive, phrase for the traditional rigidly
syllogistic structure. The *Oratio*, too, makes a studied effort,
and a successful one, to avoid any logical structure or ordered
reasoning. It is rhetorical, emotional, repetitive, and defies
more than a casual outline into major groupings. Certain of
the ideas, particularly the more dramatic ones are rephrased

and used again to press home the central theme. Any condensation as the following must lose the force and much of the flavor of the whole piece which actually approaches a very natural expression where one might have reason to expect a stilted bit of school rhetoric. Celtis' vigorous and colorful personality shines through everywhere. He begins on a modest note but soon becomes characteristically aggressive:

I would not have considered it exceptional, most worthy fathers and most admirable young men, that I as a German and your fellow countryman should be able to speak to you in Latin, if those former geniuses of our Germany were still flowering and that age had returned when our ambassadors are said to have spoken Greek rather than Latin. But since through the evil of the centuries and the ravages of time not only among you but even in Italy, the mother and venerable parent of letters, all the splendor of literature has at last become extinct and passed away and all noble studies have been beaten down and routed by barbarian movements, I am not at all sure that with my slowness of mind and the weakness of my powers I can speak to you satisfactorily in Latin. . . But I have chosen rather to offend you with stammering than to pass by in silence my love for you and for the republic of letters. . . I have decided, moreover, that I could speak to you on no subject more worthy or pleasant than encouraging you to virtue and the study of the liberal arts. For thereby true glory, immortal fame, and happiness can be so easily obtained in this brief life of ours! No one among you ought to be found so phlegmatic and lazy that he would not consider it a beautiful, excellent, and magnificent thing to work for these great ends which are able to make one truly blessed. . . For these ends wise men finally won divine honors and will in the future have an immortal name and being highly venerated and cultivated by all posterity they have come to be known by the name of philosophers. . . I shall be satisfied and more than satisfied, Oh German men and most brilliant youths, if whatever I say today even with faltering diction would succeed in adding, inculcating, and burning into your minds, so to speak, some stimulus of glory and virtue so that you may hold immortality before your eyes above all things. . . I can hardly describe with what labors and vigils one must reflect and sweat over these two things, that is, over the writings of the ancient philosophers, poets and orators. They alone have described for us how to live the good and blessed life and have presented Nature, the parent of human kind and the cycle of all things, as an example and mirror of life to be emulated. . . Moreover, though it is possible for all these things to be done by others, nevertheless, somehow the power to stir compassion and to rouse or repress the spirit lies in the hand of the orator and poet. . .

Noble men and lofty-minded youth, to whom because of the ancestral virtue and that unconquerable strength of Germany the imperium of Italy has passed, who crowd into this university above all others in Germany, enrich it and become its ornament and decoration. I exhort you to devote yourselves first of all to those studies which will render your minds more refined and cultured and summon you away from the way of the common herd to give yourselves over to higher pursuits. Hold before your eyes the true nobility of spirit remembering that you bring not credit but dishonor to our empire if you neglect the study of letters in favor of raising horses and dogs and seeking ecclesiastical prebends. . . Emulate, noble men, the ancient Roman nobility, which, after succeeding to the empire of the Greeks, took over also all their wisdom and eloquence to such an extent that it is a question whether it equalled all the Greek inventions and apparatus of learning or surpassed them. So you also having taken over the empire of the Italians ought to reject shameful barbarism and become enthusiasts for the Roman arts. Remove that old infamy of the Germans in Greek, Latin, and Hebrew writers who ascribe to us drunkenness, inhumanity, cruelty, and every other evil approximating bestiality and irrationality. . . Cast away, high-minded gentlemen, cast away and purge those robberies which they commemorate as proofs of virtue among us! . . . It should cause us shame, noble men, that certain modern historians [Sabbellicus], publishing new *Decads* and glorying in having equaled the ancient Roman empire, should refer to our most famous princes merely as "the barbarians". . . So powerful has been that old and inexpiable hatred between us and that ancient discord of our deities that it would, because of mutual hostility, inevitably have led to slaughter, if provident nature had not separated us by the Alps and by peaks reaching up to the stars. Let us be ashamed, I beg, that having engaged in and won many memorable wars in Hungary, France, and Italy and against that most inhuman tyrant of Asia who wallows in Christian blood, no one can be found among you today who will preserve for all eternity the deeds accomplished by German courage...

Take up again, Oh German men, that old spirit of yours with which you so many times were a terror and specter to the Romans and turn your eyes to the four corners of Germany and gather together her torn and scattered territories. We should be ashamed, ashamed, that we have placed the yoke of slavery on our nation and that we are paying tributes and tariffs to foreign and barbarian kings. Oh free and mighty people, oh noble and brave nation clearly worthy of the Roman imperium, our renowned seaport is held by the Pole and the gateway of our ocean by the Dane! In the East, moreover, very powerful peoples labor as slaves, the Bohemians, the Moravians, the Slovaks, and the Silesians who all live as if separated from the body of our Germany. I may add also the Transylvanian Saxons who use our culture and language. To the west is France which is so friendly and generous toward us because of the immortal virtue and incredible wisdom of Philipp, count palatine of the Rhine, who rules both banks of this renowned river and will always govern them with a fortunate rule

> While the pole rotates the stars
> and the winds bear down on the shores.

From the south, what is more, I cannot say with what a distinguished servitude we are suppressed and out of that ancient and accursed avarice for the increase of luxuries new colonies are always being established through which our land is being depleted of its wonderful resources while we who are ourselves needy pay out to others...

I return to you, oh well-born youths, and admonish you above all that you remember before you embark upon the learning of the law that a knowledge of many things is necessary for you, because that discipline is able to teach nothing except mere opinion. Moreover, the philosophers and the first theological poets, if one may believe antiquity, called men who were then wandering nomads away from the dens and caves of wild beasts into cities and social dwellings, through eloquence made their crude minds more tender, taught them religion and the fear and worship of the gods

and then ruled them by laws and institutions. Therefo.
among you will doubt, oh most distinguished fathers, that
the study of law great labor ought first be devoted to true
losophy and especially to those studies by which eloquence ca.
acquired, which you will confess to be very necessary for t.
purpose. . .

By a narrow margin of the fates by chance, because of the series
of events and the dregs of this last time, the empire grows old and
all philosophy is neglected and we prostitute our servile spirits to
unworthy complaining and put them out for a mercenary wage. . .
And these are the seminal reasons, I say it with great bitterness,
why our princes look with strange eyes on learning and always
remain unlearned and why they are held up to ridicule by others
and laughed at truly as barbarians, because in such a fortunate time
they neglect the noble arts and their proponents. . . Even among
our bishops and, if I may use the ancient word, among the sacred
*flamens* to whom the care and protection of letters ought by right
belong, there is so much contempt and undervaluation of letters. . .
Italian luxury and fierce cruelty in extorting pernicious silver
have corrupted us so badly that it would have been much more
holy and sacred for us to live such a rude forest life, as when we
lived within the limits of continence, than to have adopted the
instruments of epicureanism and luxury which are never satisfied
and to have taken over foreign customs. . . Nor will I suggest any
other cause for the continued flourishing of Italy than that the
people surpass us in no other good fortune than the love of letters
and their promotion. Thereby they dominate other peoples as if
by arms and gain their admiration by their genius and industry. . .
The foundations of religion cannot be better grounded and maintained by any better person than by a true philosopher. . .

Let no one try to contradict me by citing the multitude of our
universities of which no less than fourteen are found among us and
say that because of them barbarism has been eliminated and that
counsel has been taken and a way opened up for good morals and
honest arts. Because, although the common crowd flatters us agree-
ably who have the titles of master and doctor among whom, I say
it with tears, you will find few who follow after a true knowledge
of things and seek to hold to research into nature and also to the
purity of the Latin language. For in our studies of such things, not

to say playing at them, those who are held to be infamous who reveal the work of nature and the wisdom of its Governor by mathematical truth and who go a little further into things than the common crowd. Philosophy is so much debased and bankrupted by such men who have deformed the most beautiful majesty of nature into incorporeal concepts, monstrous abstractions and inane Chimaeras, as if they were poets. . . Moreover, if the common crowd understood certain secrets, like the philosophers, it would be difficult to repress their impetuosity. . . Although even among those who labor under my weakness taking the name of poet or orator there are those who neglect every precept of philosophy and eloquence and stretch every nerve of their genius for a certain futile loquacity and to nourish the minds of the youths with strange phantasies. . . We persecute with hatred those who bewail and regret our outmoded system of teaching and propose new ideas from the true Roman system and compel our ancient grammarians to learn the fundamentals of the Greek language and to wail again in the cradle with the infants of grammar. . . Those of us who desire to seem more learned in doctrine delay with puerile contentions of terms and quiddities over which, as on the rocks of the Sirens, we grow old and die. . . This our everyday philosophy has taught us with its worthless seeds of empty words for which we neglect the most pure and pleasing writers of our religion. We will not be able to achieve anything magnificant, high and excellent as long as we follow lesser objectives, as if certain fundamentals of our religion were not to be found in Plato and Pythagoras and other leading philosophers by whom the most beautiful union of the light of nature and of grace is perceived. But of this another time.

Turn, then, Germans, turn to more cultured studies which philosophy and eloquence alone can teach you. . . Under the influence of the things to which sublime admiration is due [poetry, drama, music, oratory], the beauty and polish of words, the minds of the youths are easily moulded into shape. And at a more robust age, when the young mind has been prepared by these beginnings and their power of thought made sounder, they are then able, better instructed and prepared, to undertake the reading of more weighty philosophers and orators. From these, finally, they can rise to their own creative writing and the sublimity of the poetic discipline and its imagery. And at last they will win the praises of illustrious authors by writing histories and poems and will secure thereafter immortality for themselves and glory and praise for their fatherland. I have spoken.

This melange presents at least the most important ideas of the *Oratio*. Two basic emphases are discernible, the attempt to formulate a new educational ideal and the powerful drive of national patriotism, mainly romantic and cultural, but with implied political overtones. The essence of his reform is the development of a new cultural course of studies which would be a synthesis of mathematical and astronomical studies, of revised grammatical instruction including Latin and Greek, of geography and history, classical, but above all German history, of rhetoric, poetry, and music. All of these come under the proper direction of the poet-philosopher. It must be emphasized that he does not expressly attack the arts course and its aristotelian orientation, but he wishes to revitalize and broaden it through his more universal discipline, his poetic philosophy. He no longer appreciated the original purpose of the arts course as the preparation for scholastic theology and favored therefore a more general secular education on the pattern of Italian classicism. Not that he was overtly anti-religious. On the contrary, he expressly states that true philosophy alone could be the basis of religion. His poetic philosophy is clearly a broad system of thought embracing knowledge human and divine, just as Plato and Pythagoras combine "the light of nature with that of grace." Indeed, Celtis states specifically that this method of knowledge includes "revealing the work of nature and the wisdom of its director by mathematical truth." And the goal of this new *via* of virtue, for all practical purposes a secular ethic? "Blessed immortality."

His romantic nationalism is evident even in his discussion of philosophy in the *Oratio* where he attributes a measure of national decadence to the effects of scholasticism. He seems to be addressing especially the boys of the better families, many of whom would naturally be intended for the study of law, and singles them out for special mention. He warns against the danger of law becoming a mere trade and against the neglect of letters in favor of mere law books, as had Gerald de Barri at Paris around 1200. This is a perennial problem, but Celtis sees it as all the more serious, because the fatherland is in need of philosopher-statesmen in its present plight. The endless civil war and strife for trivial gain must come to an end. With the *Oratio*, Celtis published a hymn, "Ad divam dei genitricem pro pace et concordia principum Germanorum." The youth must rise, cast off foreign tyranny, restore the old borders, and write anew for posterity the history of their Germany.[6]

Together with the *Oratio*, Celtis published an ode to his young friend, Sigismund Fusilius of Breslau, whom he had known for two years in Cracow.[7] In a prosaic systematic way Celtis checks off the areas of knowledge which the young philosopher, that is, a young humanist ought to know. He emphasizes Roman grammar first, then astronomy, geography, history, contempt of fortune, and moral philosophy. "Find out," Celtis charges him, "with soaring mind the causes of individual things." Once again the piece concludes with the essence of his moral philosophy, an admonition to follow the path of virtue to the heavenly home.

> *Scorn the favor of unstable fortune*
> *And learn to bear hard blows.*
> *All your days will thus pass for you*
> *In blessed time.*
>
> *Rise and high-minded mount up*
> *The straight and narrow path of virtue*
> *Which alone enables you*
> *To lead a secure life.*

*Virtue alone promising pleasant honors*
*Offers blessedness in the heavenly abode*
*And removes fear of the black shadows*
*In the Stygian prison.*

Such virtue leads to a heavenly city not far from that of the eighteenth-century philosophers. Was this poetic culture ethically sound enough, intellectually pure enough, religiously deep enough, actually sincere enough for a generation which was in greater travail than Celtis could know?

A few days after delivering his "Inaugural Address" Celtis abandoned the *cathedra* and took to the road once more. The summer semester was not yet over and his six months appointment had not as yet run out, but Celtis had his fill of teaching for the time being and decided to visit his close friend Johannes Tolhopf, canon of the Cathedral of Regensburg. The note with which he informed Tucher of his departure is characteristic.[8]

To Sixtus Tucher, my dearest brother, so to speak:

I shall depart today for Regensburg and from there go to Linz in order to greet my friends in the pleasant court of our emperor. Though if by some chance or opportunity it should happen that I go down to Vienna and my travel should draw me away from you beyond the termination of our vacation, you may be certain and full of hope for my return. I have no doubt that you and my other friends will see to the extension of my stipend. Vale.

Conradus Celtis

There is no hint that he left because of opposition to his humanist oration. Rather, every indication is that he was feeling the confidence inspired by an easy success. He stayed only very briefly in Regensburg. At Linz he renewed his friendship with members of the imperial court dating from his poet's crowning in 1487, especially with Krachenberger (Graccus Pierius), the secretary of the imperial chancellery, who had written to him in April excusing his long neglect and calling on Stiborius, Reuchlin, and Petrus Bonomus to witness to his concern for Celtis. He doubtless also met Fuchsmagen once more, a leading jurist and statesman. Krachenberger, as a colleague of Bernhard Perger, superintendent of the University of Vienna, was a friend especially worth cultivating and Celtis did not fail to do so. By September 21 he was already in Vienna, traveling there perhaps with some members of the highly mobile court. In Vienna, Celtis made a number of good friends who became his enthusiastic supporters.

Nothing came of an effort to secure for Celtis a position at Vienna, largely because an influential faction at the university including the Superintendent Perger favored calling an Italian humanist. Celtis returned to Regensburg and may even have paid Ingolstadt the honor of a brief visit, making a digression to Nuremberg around December, before returning for a longer stay with his friend Tolhopf in Regensburg. Meanwhile Celtis was negotiating through Tucher for the renewal of his appointment. The whole proceeding is revealed in a series of highly entertaining letters not without parallel in present-day academic politics reflecting his rationalizations, his superiority and disdain for the petty officials of Ingolstadt, his offense at their lack of appreciation. He was furious with the "old hack and beet eater" now occupying the chair rightfully his. He remained that winter with Tolhopf and to earn a livelihood accepted in February the rectorship of the cathedral school at Regensburg to the amazement of his Vienna friends.[9]

Tolhopf, a canon at the cathedral, proved to be a most congenial comrade. But nearby Nuremberg was more attractive to Celtis with its circle of good friends and wealthy burghers than Regensburg. Celtis hoped it might also have something more tangible to offer.

# Nuremberg and the *Norimberga*

T HE DAY had not yet arrived for Nuremberg when Hutten would hail it as the first city to open its doors to good learning, Melanchthon call it another Athens, or Luther pronounce it the eye and ear of Germany. But even in the 1490's it was more sympathetic to new ideas than many cities in the North. This does not mean that humanism was to win an early or an easy victory, for the ruling aristocracy was basically conservative and resisted innovations on this level. Most representatives of humanism in Nuremberg were in fact not Nurembergers. But all agreed with Aeneas Silvius that Nuremberg was the center of Germany and of Europe.[1]

At least compared with Regensburg, Nuremberg could offer the company of a larger number of prosperous citizens kindly disposed toward humanism and toward Celtis. The prime mover in this circle of friends was the magnanimous patrician and councilor, Sebald Schreyer. He and his friends felt they needed the inspiration and assistance of Celtis in undertaking a number of literary projects. Peter Danhauser, a jurist interested in Roman law, invited Celtis to Nuremberg for the showing of the imperial relics at Easter time. Celtis accepted and remained in Nuremberg through the summer and almost to the end of the year 1493.

Celtis was hardly the man for the ambitious publishing then under discussion. He left behind him a trail of unfinished projects, yet another sign of his lack of discipline and organization. Celtis himself was contemplating the publication of a Roman mythology and an illustrated edition of Ovid's *Fasti*. Nothing came of the idea. Perhaps with the mythology Celtis had in mind participation in the *Archetypus liberalium artium* which Peter Danhauser was planning. To this grand but unfulfilled enterprise, Celtis contributed not a thing. He likewise failed to respond to Schreyer's suggestion that he correct and enlarge Hartmann Schedel's *Liber Chronicarum*.[2] Celtis was busy with a piece which could be completed with dispatch and which promised a quicker return, a description of Nuremberg and a tribute to its wise council. He needed money, of course. Danhauser had paid one debt for him and urged him to pay better attention to his affairs in the future. Surely such a work would be well received and well rewarded. Moreover, his friends urged him to undertake this labor of love.

There was ample precedent both classic and contemporary for this type of city description. The city state structure of antiquity and of the Italian Renaissance lent itself to this type of writing. Leonardo Bruni's *Laudatio Florentinae urbis* was itself an imitation of Aristides' *De Laudibus Athenarum*. The oldest work of this kind in Germany was Albrecht von Eyb's *Ad laudem et commendationem civitatis Bambergae*, 1452. Nor had Nuremberg itself been neglected. Celtis posed as the first man to use Latin in lauding the city and felt called for the task. Actually the Nuremberg chronicle of the Benedictine monk Sigismund Meisterlin and the world chronicle of Schedel including a description of Nuremberg had been written in Latin, though both had been quickly translated into German. Celtis must have known them. In 1492, Georg Alt wrote two small treatises, a *Descriptio Nurmbergae* in Latin and one in German, though neither was published. There are many correspondences between the Latin version and Celtis' own work, but largely in such matters as the descriptive content, the praise of the city constitution, its spirituality, charities, fortifications, where the similarity could be derived directly from the subject matter. Moreover, in his description of the spirituality of the city and the patrician government he was close to two Nuremberg poets, Hans Rosenplüt and Kunz Has, whose poems on Nuremberg were published in 1490 and 1492. But, as a matter of fact, Celtis' major source was the city itself which he examined with a keen eye and described with a new freshness and lucidity in an excellent Latin, his only prose work aside from the *Oratio*. He far transcended his predecessors.[3]

Almost a decade intervened between the first work on the *Norimberga* in 1493 and its ultimate publication in 1502. The story of Celtis' machinations and procrastinations with the *Norimberga* underlines some major weaknesses of his character. Georg Alt's translation of the piece was speedy, though that was its only virtue, for he finished it before the year 1495 was out. Meanwhile the none-too-delicate negotiations for a fitting reward from the council continued. At last, in 1502, Hieronymus Höltzel at Nuremberg published the *Norimberga* in an omnibus volume of his various works. Celtis received his reward—twenty gulden, of light weight.

Celtis indeed deserved better treatment from the council. The *Norimberga* was in its genre a masterpiece. One of the strong points of Renaissance prose was the description of surroundings, whether it was Petrarch depicting the Cologners, Poggio, the Badeners, or Aeneas Silvius the Rhine cities. There was a drive toward greater realism. Celtis' description of Nuremberg was an excellent demonstration of this development. It was the ripe fruit of his keen and surprisingly precise observation. With warm interest and great skill, he portrayed in sixteen chapters of varying length the geographical setting, the structure of the city, the public and private buildings, the characteristics of the people, the religious life, the civic government, and the material prosperity of the city. The range of subjects and his penetration were truly remarkable. No patriot could have concluded this tribute to the city with a more stirring prayer: "So we beseech you, oh immortal gods, if our prayer can yet avail something, that you preserve and defend our city in its prosperity, welfare, and lasting stability. May you the guardian tutelary gods, rulers of the fates of lands and cities, preserve with protective hand the blessings of good fortune as long as the firmament bears the stars and the wind moves the waves!"

The *Norimberga* tells us almost as much about Celtis as about the city. His description is a living conception, the product of an independent personality not bound by the learned dullness of his predecessors. In the initial chapters he soberly informs us that he has done research in books and histories, but there is almost no evidence for it. The strength of the piece lies in its warm human interest. The descriptions of the spring festivals before the gates, the joy with which the young and old walk happily in a summer evening, the sport events and city carnivals are nothing less than poetic prose. The smallest details do not escape him, the dress of the nuns, the ceremony in which an initiate is declared dead to the world, the changing of the guard. He relates with great appeal how the old Emperor Frederick invited all the boys under ten to the castle for Lebkuchen. He includes, of course, his own crowning on the fortress hill. He describes the dread famine of 1491, the companies of weak, emaciated peasants begging before the church doors, the longing for death with which the thief greeted the rope as his only relief from sorrow. Nor is the *Norimberga* a mere panegyric, for he criticizes the beer and gives a fictional account of how it was made, chides the frequent drinking bouts of the rowdy set, observes the tendency to artificial overpoliteness, and regrets the neglect of the public library.

The weaknesses stem largely from the tendency to exaggerate and the humanist mistletoe appended here and there. His estimates of 4,000 births a year and a total population of 52,000 is quite impossible, considering that at the same time Strassburg is known to have had a population of only 16,000 and Basel 15,000. When in 1806 the city entered the kingdom of Bavaria, it had only 25,000 inhabitants. Nor does the effect ring true when he calls the monks druids, the furnace workers cyclopses, misses the pictures of Apollo and the Muses in the commons, or finds the sound of church bells strange. Moreover, in a city which already contained great treasures, Celtis had a complete blind spot for fine arts, a weakness which he shared with Hutten, Mutian, Erasmus, and many other literary humanists.

The *Norimberga* reveals an essentially conservative social mentality. Celtis supports the sumptuary laws and medieval guild regulations. He approves of the aristocratic government and relates a story which is highly illustrative. Frederick III riding back from his crowning as emperor and seeing the pressing masses of people asked the councilors riding next to him how it was possible to rule the masses in peace, prevent uprisings and disturbances. "By good words and heavy corporal punishment and fines," answered the councilor. For good free citizens mild words suffice, for the masses, punishment. A worthy saying which rulers of other states could emulate, comments Celtis. He was aware of the hypertrophy of the new capitalism. He saw that some citizens "live not from heaven and earth, but only of money." In the drive for profits the Nurembergers were "like bees in the flowers looking everywhere for treasures and riches to bring back to their city."[4] But he saw it only to pass on to other interests. In his effort to praise the spirituality of Nuremberg he did not discern the religious restlessness even then evident which later led Nuremberg as one of the first cities into the Reformation movement.

Toward the nobility Celtis was consistently hostile. There is little hint from him that the nobles took to the new learning before the burghers. To a young student of his at Ingolstadt who came from a noble family and felt quite despondent in the drab chambers of his castle at Topfheim Celtis wrote:

> *You alone among nobles, brilliant one,*
> *Always remain a friend to Muses.*
> *So that blessed you invest an ancient family*
> *With a really true nobility.*
> *This is a rare glory in Teuton lands*
> *That nobles created with ancient blood*
> *Should have inborn concerns*
> *For the muses and highest wisdom.*[5]

"Why boast of noble ancestry if you are ignorant and lost in vices?" asked the learned peasant's son in lines reminiscent of Voltaire's sentiment, "Whoever serves his country well has no need of ancestors." There were basic similarities in many social attitudes of the humanists and the savants of the century of light.

The fine qualities of the *Norimberga* make it all the more regrettable that Celtis did not complete the work for which he intended the *Norimberga* to serve as a kind of prelude, his *Germania illustrata*. The idea for this major work was undoubtedly derived from Flavio Biondo's *Italia illustrata*. It was to be a book designed to illustrate his Germany, its past, its geographic setting, its cities, and its people. Just as Tacitus' *Germania* was to serve as a preliminary study, so the *Norimberga* with its long chapter on the Hercynian forest was to be a kind of trial or prelude for the *Germania illustrata*. But the same failings which so long delayed the publication of the *Norimberga* prevented also the progress and completion of a larger work.

While in Nuremberg, Celtis did complete, however, another tribute to the city—an ode to its patron saint, St. Sebaldus. One is reminded of the good taste with which Erasmus refused the invitation of Albert of Mainz to write in humanist style the lives of the saints. Such inhibitions would not have restrained Celtis. At the request of his *de facto* patron, Sebald Schreyer, in 1493 he composed the poem relating the life of the saint. It was then published in Basel, probably late in the year 1494 or early in 1495, in Latin type with a woodcut in the center of the text showing the saint standing on a pedestal under a façade with the arms of France and Denmark above and those of Celtis and Schreyer below.[6] This woodcut may very well have been from the workshop of Michael Wohlgemut. Celtis may then have lost the woodcut, for the next year a second edition of the poem appeared, this time with a new picture of Sebaldus, this time with vines replacing the gothic arch overhead and the stiff lines gone leading some to believe that the second illustration may have come not from the old master Wohlgemut, but from his young understudy Dürer. Artists were at least useful to the humanists as book illustrators.

Before the end of the year Celtis was to make the most sensational book find of his life: the codex of the dramas of Roswitha, the nun of Gandersheim, who in the tenth century had written legends and dramas in the spirit of the Ottonian Renaissance. In the *Oratio* Celtis had decried neglect in Germany of the precious stores of books which were left shut up in prison, covered with dust, untouched, and scarcely safe from rain. Italians like Poggio had, of course, been busy searching through the monastic libraries of Germany. Now Celtis enlisting the support of his friends undertook a similar search for treasures of the German past. Near the end of 1493, in the Benedictine monastery of St. Emmeram in Regensburg where he was once more visiting his friend Tolhopf, he made his great find, Roswitha's six dramas. What a find! Here was a playwright and a woman who in the Middle Ages held aloft the light of classic learning writing in the manner of Terence. Celtis was elated. He borrowed the codex from the prior, Laurentius Aicher, promising through Friedrich Rosenritter, an honorable citizen of Nuremberg, to return it, which, of course, he never did.[7] He shared his joy with his friends instead, sending the codex first to Sixtus Tucher in Ingolstadt. He next sent it to his friend Trithemius, the abbot of Sponheim, so that he might have a copy made, but he wrote back on April 11, 1495, from Frankfurt, that he had not yet had it copied, but that he had discussed with Amerbach the possibility of having it printed.[8] When the priceless manuscript had been returned, Celtis still made no copy, but wrote his corrections into the text, added his observations, and a table of contents and turned it finally in 1501 to a printer where it picked up a few additional ink smudges and thumb prints. He had very little antiquarian reverence or even practical caution about him.

Meanwhile, Riedner, the old poet, had vacated his position in Ingolstadt and Celtis went to Ingolstadt probably in February 1494, to become the regular professor of the humanities. On May 7 he was duly registered in the matriculation book. He rented a house and began lecturing again, this time on Ovid. The philosophical faculty received him none too cordially and when he asked permission to use the library, it was granted only on the condition that he promise to abide by the rules of the faculty and cease to criticize the other professors. That his responsibilities as a *lector ordinarius* rendered him less independent could hardly be expected.

He soon demonstrated that his new position had not tamed him, for late that very summer he left Ingolstadt for a trip to the Rhine. In a cutting ode, doubtless only privately circulated, he explained why he was leaving the Ingolstadters. He could no longer bear the company of the beet eaters who had no wine, no hills, and no river except the Danube, therefore he was seeking the Rhine to enjoy good wine and the company of learned men. He may have traveled up the Danube toward Freiburg im Breisgau, the home of Ulrich Zasius, famed as a humanist and specialist in Roman law. Zasius congratulated Celtis upon the penetration of his humanist thought world into Freiburg and urged him to see him again.[9] Celtis in turn dedicated an ode to Zasius praising his work on Roman law and declaring that he will thereby oppose the depraved arts of the priests, will purge Rome, and help the centuries to return to the ancient golden age. From Freiburg he moved on to Basel, possibly bringing his Sebaldus ode along to leave here for publication. In Basel he made friends of Johannes Silbernberger, a professor of jurisprudence, and Hartmann von Eppingen, a prosperous canon who was his host and a kind of Maecenas to the humanists there. He apparently brought his Roswitha codex along to show his new friends. Celtis praised the Swiss as the only free people in Germany and gained on his trip a vivid impression of the beautiful Rhine valley past Reichenau and Constance to Basel.[10] Celtis may have included in the Rhine trip also a trip to Sponheim and a visit with Trithemius, for he apparently introduced him to the study of Greek sometime during the year 1494.

It was high time that he return to the University. Criticism of his negligence was mounting. His friend, the librarian of the Regensburg monastery, Erasmus Australis, warned him against further frivolities:

I beg you emphatically as much as it is possible for you to be concerned about staying at one place and location and carefully and thoughtfully to stop that wandering around which results more from your levity and the changeableness of your disposition than from necessity. For I hear that not a little talk may arise, and rather already has arisen, because you have hardly for six weeks concerned yourself with your main task of lecturing, for which you after all were hired and that it therefore could easily happen that you may be removed from your regular teaching post.[11]

This sobering admonition, or possibly poor traveling conditions, kept Celtis in Ingolstadt through the winter, except possibly for an occasional visit to nearby Nuremberg where his friend Schreyer was at the time busy having the walls of his house decorated in the Italian manner with pictures of the gods, wise men, and Muses. His perseverance comes as quite a surprise, but fate was soon to intervene. That dreaded scourge, the plague, struck in the summer of 1495. The doctors were among the first to flee and Celtis was not far behind.

# The Rhenish Sodality

T HE GREAT emphasis traditionally placed upon the individualism of the Renaissance man has tended to obscure the conformity of the individual humanist to the group pattern and the strong tendency toward association evident particularly among the northern humanists. Classical antiquity, of course, had set ample precedent for academies and schools of thought. The Italian Renaissance in turn developed associations of learned men on the classic pattern, especially in Florence, Naples, and Rome. But in the North, where the humanists were in less immediate contact with the remains of the classical civilization, they felt more strongly the need to establish a union of like-minded men. For such a communal movement the gregarious Celtis had a special talent. Unlike Erasmus, who as an emperor worked best alone and at a distance from his public, Celtis could work as a *Primus inter pares* and only in a large company did he feel really in his element. He became the moving spirit in the closer union of the German humanists and his name became a symbol of the new fraternity. Around the turn of the century there was not a single humanist of any importance who was not in some way connected with Celtis.

That Celtis should seek the Rhine when fleeing the plague in Ingolstadt was only natural. He was received in Heidelberg by a good friend from his first stay there, Johannes Vigilius

(Wacker). Vigilius was a professor of jurisprudence at Heidelberg University and was active in the service of both the Elector Philipp of the Palatinate, and Dalberg the Bishop of Worms and chancellor of the Palatinate. Vigilius was a practical man of affairs, generous and expansive. It was probably through his influence that Celtis was appointed tutor of the sons of the Elector Philipp and so gained access to the court circle in the Heidelberg castle. His home was a hospice not only for Celtis but was a center for the humanists of the whole upper Rhine. Celtis years later dedicated to him a warmly human ode celebrating his preference of learning to riches, and the warm comradery prevailing in his home, the wine, the jokes, the dice, the song, the laughter, and the joys of Venus, suggesting thereby one reason why more serious scholarship did not come out of the Heidelberg circle. "Oh, how pleasant were those days when we pursued together our common studies and our hearts glowed with mutual affection!"[1]

In this milieu Celtis with his imaginative flair and dramatic touch was able to actualize an idea which he had harbored for a long time, an association of learned men for the advancement of the new literary culture, a *Sodalitas litteraria*. The precise date of its founding is uncertain, but it seems likely that it was organized, to the extent that it was ever organized, during the autumn of 1495.[2] The first certain date for the origin of the sodality is December 8, 1495, when Heinrich von Bünau, a Saxon nobleman wrote Celtis from Worms to thank him for the invitation to join the "Academia Platonica." Bishop Johannes von Dalberg was naturally elected president of the academy and maintained his prerogatives until his death eight years later. Indeed, upon his death the society disintegrated completely. Vigilius' house served as the central meeting place and the scene of festive banquets of the *sodales*. He was the host of the sodality and Dalberg's right-hand man.

The sodality was very loosely organized. Dalberg made some rules for the members, but they were largely for display purposes only. The membership was flexible and it may be doubted whether there was a fixed list of members at all. In the one collection of names which might approximate such a membership list in formality, the epigrams contributed by members of the literary sodality for all Germany to the publication of Roswitha's works in 1501, not all the members of the Rhenish Sodality were included, but some are named who were never active in other projects.[3] The Dalberg circle made up the nucleus of the Rhenish Sodality with most of the members in Heidelberg and its vicinity, but with a few in more distant monasteries and other cities. The sodality included a large number of churchmen, secular and regular, as well as doctors, jurists, mathematicians, rhetoricians, and poets. It represented a spectrum of humanist development also from the very conservative basically pious interest in classical literature, poetry and rhetoric, as a new mode of expression for the old ideas to the more radical interest in new causes intellectual and patriotic.

The immediate Heidelberg group present either during Celtis' residence there or shortly thereafter included several interesting personalities besides Dalberg and Vigilius. Jodocus Gallus, a friend of Agricola, was one of the leading theology professors at the University, renowned for his lectures on the logic and physics of Aristotle. Jakob Dracontius, a premonstratensian monk, was a special favorite of Dalberg whom he celebrated repeatedly in Latin odes. Two legists also belonged to the group; Dietrich Rysicheus, who had received his doctorate of laws in Italy and was to become a professor at Ingolstadt and assessor of the *Reichskammergericht;* and Heinrich Spiesz (Cuspidianus), of a noble family, a jurist who followed Celtis back to Ingolstadt as his student.

But a man destined to fame in his own right was Johann Reuchlin. He had not at this time as yet achieved special distinction. He had been busy at Sponheim teaching Trithemius Greek, was prominent at the court of Elector Philipp, and later succeeded Celtis and Adam Werner of Themar as the tutor of the Elector's children. His presence in the sodality serves as a reminder that the increasing solidarity of the humanists might serve also a polemic end. He and Krachenberger, the imperial secretary, composed a poem to Celtis celebrating his high standing with the Muses. Celtis on his part later wrote an ode to Reuchlin or Capnion, the philosopher and interpreter of three languages.[4] How often there at the Rhine, reminisced Celtis, we read whatever the Latins, Greeks, and Hebrews sang and discussed what the lawgiver Moses brought forth in sacred volume. Venerated in Tübingen and Basel, you mastered the knowledge of three ancient peoples and wrote copiously comic farces. "Hence the Bishop celebrated throughout the cities of the Rhine, who cherishes the comrades, will support you, and by my lyrics you will gain a name for all eternity." It was a generous offer quite worthy of Celtis.

The sodality drew its members also from monasteries and other cities along the upper Rhine. One of the most learned of these commuting members was Trithemius, Abbot of the Benedictine monastery of Sponheim. Celtis was among the humanists who beat a path to Sponheim. During his Heidelberg stay he confirmed his friendly relationship with Trithemius, a bond which lasted until his death.

Celtis also attempted to draw the Alsatian pedagogue, Jakob Wimpheling, closer to the Heidelberg circle. Wimpheling had left the University in 1483 to become the cathedral preacher at Speyer. He illustrated better than any other the impact of humanism on a man who was basically a late scholastic theologian. To the invitation to join the Heidelberg circle of friends, Wimpheling responded with a shy demurer. He could not travel in mid-winter for reasons of health. Moreover, what should a crow do among the nightingales or an owl among the falcons?

The Heidelberg circle drew into its orbit a miscellany of lesser men with varying degrees of permanence. The casual nature of the whole organization meant a fluid and nebulous membership. The sodality began to disintegrate with Dalberg's resignation as chancellor and the removal of his residence to Ladenburg. His death in 1503 and the war of succession between Bavaria and the Palatinate shattered what little cohesion remained in the Rhenish Sodality after the departure of Celtis for the Danube.

What the Rhenish Sodality lacked in formal organization it provided in the dramatic flourish of its accouterments. Celtis himself loved ceremony and never tired of referring to his crowning with the poet's laurel. Fascinated by numerical symmetries, the sodality placed great emphasis upon the importance of the threefold name, the three sacred languages, and the threefold philosophy. They all classicized their Germanic cognomens in the most pedantic fashion. Many merely added a classic ending to their names. Others were harder pressed. Eitelwolf vom Stein, the renowned patron of Reuchlin and Hutten and a member of Celtis' larger literary sodality, rechristened himself Ololikos de Stein. Krachenberger became Graccus Pierius. Spieszhaym emerged as Cuspinian. Some men outside of Celtis' immediate circle achieved even greater philological coups. A Wolfgang became Lupambulus, Bredekopp became Laticephalus, and Wodka became, admirably, Abstemius. Some names even in their final form left something to be desired, notably Mommerlochus and Gockenschnabelius. A few men of greater substance, as Reuchlin, who was solemnly renamed Capnion (καπνός, smoke) by the Venetian

Ermolao Barbaro, preferred their German name to the new affectation. Equally as strained was the conceit of comparing each other with the heroes of antiquity, as when Petrus Schott praised Bohuslaus von Hassenstein higher than Homer, Virgil, and Ovid and when Bohuslaus reciprocated by declaring that Schott overshadowed Homer, Aristotle, and Cicero, or when Locher compared Brant's *Narrenschiff* with the Homeric poems.[5] To his credit it must be said that Celtis had the good taste not to do this himself.

Theoretically the promotion of the three sacred languages was one of the stipulations for admission to the sodality. This was sheer bluff, for few members of the sodality were at all proficient in Greek and only Reuchlin achieved any prowess worthy of mention in Hebrew. Celtis himself claimed credit as the first to introduce to Germany all three languages.[6] As early as 1491 he had compiled a handbook of the essentials of Greek grammar, giving an overview in tables of the declension of nouns and conjugation of verbs. This crude compilation came to be known as his Greek grammar and was sought after as an aid to study by the comrades.[7] But Celtis was a poet not a scholar, and his confession to Nicolaus Gelonus that having been captured by love he could not pay attention to the Greek muses was as much a statement of fact as a literary flourish.[8] In his contagious inspiration lay his chief contribution to Greek learning. In fact, if the achievements in Greek had equaled the interest in Greek, the whole sodality would have produced a new Periclean age.

Bohuslaus von Hassenstein celebrated Celtis for his triumph over barbarism and the grace with which he wore the triple laurel crown of Latin, Greek, and Hebrew. Actually, Celtis' knowledge of Hebrew was negligible. He made the gesture of using a few Hebrew vocables, but that was as far as it went. It is clear, however, where his sympathies if not his abilities lay and where he would have stood in the Reuchlin controversy had he lived a decade longer. The only voice of dissent, in fact, came from his peculiar friend Tolhopf, the canon of Regensburg, who angrily opposed the study of Hebrew on astrological grounds.

The sodality was dedicated also to the threefold Neoplatonic Philosophy. Celtis himself was called the "triformis philosophiae doctor." What precisely the comrades meant by this was unclear even to themselves. Formally they must have been referring to the wisdom derived from each of the three languages or to the traditional threefold division of philosophy into *philosophia naturalis, moralis, et rationalis.* Not one was given to clear conceptual thinking. The influence of Florentine Neoplatonism is evident even though elusive as to precise thought formulations. There is for one thing an aestheticizing and mythologizing tendency detectable. An inclination toward an immanentist view of God appears in the effusions of some of the more free spirits in the sodality. For the most part the strange light of the natural philosophical ideas remained but weak and uncertain. More readily identified was the Pythagorean number mysticism and the preoccupation with occult symbolism. Dalberg himself is supposed to have written a treatise "On the Secret Mysteries of Numbers." Trithemius, of course, was much concerned with astrological and demonological teachings. It was in this milieu that Reuchlin developed further his fascination with the secrets of the Cabala. In a letter to Vigilius, Reuchlin recalled the memory of the philosophic discussions of the comrades on the Aristotelian ethic which lasted late into the night. A brief insight into the daring side of the sodality's thinking emerges from Celtis' ode to the Rhenish literary sodality that with him they should prepare a banquet to celebrate the return of Phoebus from Capricorn.[9] Here is discernible the latitudinarianism, anti-clericalism, and great emphasis on fame which Celtis expressed elsewhere as well. Celtis' consistent emphasis on virtue and genius (*virtus ingeniumque*) was the main pillar of the Stoic wing in the new humanist temple.

The sodality appreciated the value of the printed word and accepted the practice, which Celtis had found helpful, of appointing members to serve as censors for each other's publications. Celtis was profuse in his praise of printing and its inventor. Now books abound, now nothing is secret any more, and all things return under a new light. One of his finest odes is dedicated to the German inventor of printing. Significantly, he coupled it with another execrating the German inventor of the cannon. It was as though he discerned both the creative and the destructive possibilities in what he regarded as newly awakened genius.[10] Within the circle of Rhenish humanism cheery optimism prevailed. In 1507 Nicolas Gerbellius, the student of Celtis, wrote to Trithemius: "I congratulate myself often on living in this glorious century in which so many remarkable men have arisen in Germany."

Heidelberg was to his taste, so Celtis procrastinated as long as possible before returning to his professorship at Ingolstadt. The plague had passed, classes were to resume on January 6, 1496, but Celtis had not yet returned. Finally in February he arrived, armed with a letter from the Count Palatine Philipp excusing Celtis for his failure to return promptly, since he had stayed on to tutor his sons, and designed to prevent any cut in salary for his late return. Contact with the Heidelberg circle continued though it was naturally reduced as time went on.

Celtis toyed with the idea of marriage after his return to Ingolstadt. He consulted his friends who treated the question in an antique manner, posing the question whether the wise should marry. His witty friend, the Nuremberg doctor Dietrich Ulsenius, who even took his own bankruptcy with equanimity, refused to take Celtis seriously. He advised against marriage, for the state of marriage is like a nest of chicks. All that are in the nest seek to crawl out and all those outside seek to crawl in. Schreyer, too, wrote from Nuremberg advising him to take a wife, if he wanted someone to torment him day and night and constantly have her glory in possessing a slave crowned by imperial hands. Humanist society in Germany had very little room for women.

Celtis very soon had occasion to regret his own record vis-à-vis womankind. In 1496 he fell victim to the first strong attack of syphilis. This siege of illness followed by another severe attack in the summer of 1498 broke his strength and he began to age very rapidly. His friend Sebald Schreyer warned Celtis against the *morbus gallicus* which was spreading through Germany and had appeared also in Nuremberg, but it was too late. Contemporary astrologers attributed the disease to the conjunction of three planets in 1494. Others, such as Celtis' Leipzig friend, Martin Pollich, denied astrological influence and acrimonious debates ensued. Present knowledge as to its origin does not extend much beyond the explanation given by the learned Dr. Pangloss to Candide that Paquette had received it through a long line of descent from one of the companions of Christopher Columbus. Celtis turned to the comforts of religion. He dismissed his classes in order to make a pilgrimage to the Bavarian shrine of Alt-Oetting and composed two votive poems imploring the aid of the Virgin in combatting the disease.

Celtis became increasingly casual about his own teaching obligations. He skipped lectures and came ill-prepared, even posting a notice that he was suspending classes, since he had been invited by a friend to enjoy the new wine. His students wrote a bitter complaint to him which he duly kept for posterity in which they lamented his way of treating them and his disregard for his classes. He accused and insulted the students with reproaches of madness. He called them, from whose stipends he was living, barbarous, stupid, and wild. Nevertheless, he continued to receive many students one of whom he left as his successor, the bumptious poet, Jakob Locher Philomusus, who began his lectures at Ingolstadt with the ringing of a bell. Humanism did not win a final triumph in Ingolstadt until the faculty statutes in 1519 set aside Alexander and the traditional texts, made the second edition of Aventine's grammar official, and made the humanist studies obligatory for all bachelor and master's degree candidates. This was over two decades after Celtis had moved on to that other city where his talents would be truly appreciated, Vienna.

6

# The Danubian Sodality

WITH the advent of Maximilian to the throne of the Holy Roman Empire, the city of Vienna entered upon one of the most brilliant periods of her long history. The death of the Hungarian conqueror Matthias Corvinus in 1490 and of the lethargic Emperor Frederick III in 1493 cleared the way for a new cultural awakening and reborn creativity. Above all, the University of Vienna benefited from the resurgence of intellectual life. It came to have the largest enrollment of all the German universities and attracted scholars from Italy also.

Since the appointment of Bernhard Perger as superintendent of the University, there had been marked progress in the advance of humanist learning. As early as the beginning of 1493 the ambitious Celtis had begun maneuvering for a position at Vienna. Negotiations were renewed in May 1496. Celtis was back in Ingolstadt and quite ready to consider any reasonable alternative. At last the council acted, and, on March 7, 1497, at Maximilian's order, addressed a flattering call to Celtis. Celtis accepted with pleasure and received the first full-time regular lectureship in poetry and rhetoric at Vienna. A very prosaic but eminently practical consideration kept Celtis in Ingolstadt another half year. He was in debt and the call to Vienna had made no mention of pay. It was not until October 1497, that Celtis saw his way clear to leave with Stiborius for Vienna.

• • 55 •

His reception in Vienna was gratifying and his first act was a sensational one. He called into being the *Sodalitas litteraria Danubiana*, an association of humanists similar to the one he had founded two years before on the Rhine. As at Heidelberg, he found the basic groundwork already laid. Like Dalberg, Johann Vitez, the Bishop of Veszprim and Vienna, served as the patron and protector of the Vienna humanists and he very naturally was elected the Prince of the new sodality. He served as a symbol personally uniting the German and Hungarian lands of the Danube. The Sodality included German, Hungarian, Bohemian, and Italian members and soon extended as far as Nuremberg and Augsburg. On December 8 the Budapest members invited Celtis to visit the Hungarian court. Celtis went in style, riding in a carriage with three span of horses in the company of Georg von Neideck, the secretary of the Hungarian royal chancellory. The comrades in Vienna and Budapest presented him with poems of greeting and congratulations which he was prompt to publish for distribution and republished later before his edition of Apuleius' *De Mundo*, *Episodia Sodalitatis litterarie Danubiane ad Conradum Celten*.

The *Episodia* provides a kind of initial membership list which is of considerable interest. The Vienna group served as the real nucleus of the sodality. Krachenberg—Joannes Graccus Pierius —commanded the lead-off position. Celtis' two mathematician friends, Stabius and Stiborius, both now at Vienna, were represented, of course. Bartholomäus Stäber (Scipio), also a professor of medicine at the University, had been active in Celtis' behalf and remained a faithful if not a prominent member of the Danubian Sodality. The fact that he was the only native of Vienna in the sodality provides an interesting commentary on Vienna as a crossroad of culture even then. Three Italians belonged also to the Vienna core of the sodality. Hieronymus Balbus, who resigned his lectureship in poetry making an opening for Celtis, did not leave Vienna until 1499 and meanwhile continued to support the humanist cause. The two brothers Petrus Bonomus, secretary of the Austrian chancellory, and Franciscus Bonomus, secretary of Queen Bianca Maria, joined in contributing a stanza of greeting. A number of the Vienna humanists were not represented: Perger, of course, but also Fuchsmagen, the doctor Johann Tichtel, and Johann Burger, probably because they had no Latin poem to submit.

The *Princeps* of the sodality, Johann Vitez, was the most prominent of the members from outside Vienna. He had served at the court of Matthias Corvinus before falling into disfavor and fleeing to Italy. In 1490 he turned to Maximilian and was now prominent as a bishop in German and Hungarian lands. Augustinus Moravus (Olomocensis), a prominent Moravian humanist, was now serving as chief secretary at the court of King Ladislaus II. Johannes Schlechta and Georg von Neideck were also serving as royal secretaries in Budapest. Julius Milius (Aemilius) had come from Italy to serve as the personal physician of the Hungarian king. Christophorus von Weitmühl was an official in the Hungarian ministry of war. Weitmühl's tutor, Johannes Sturnus, was a personal friend of Celtis and of Bohuslaus von Hassenstein. These men formed the Budapest circle of the sodality. Other friends of Celtis contributed to the *Episodia* as well.

As in the case of the Rhenish Sodality the membership was very flexible. There was apparently no formal list or fixed requirement for admission. The members congregated often in the home of Cuspinian on Singerstrasse near St. Stephen's Cathedral. On one of the walls in the court of his house, Cuspinian erected a memorial stone to the eternal memory of the Sodalitas Danubiana. On it he listed the names of the twelve men who may be considered the hard core of the sodality: Celtis, Graccus Pierius, Cuspinianus, Stabius, Ulsenius, Stiborius, Gabriel

Eubolius (Gutrater), Polymnius (Wilhelm Pülinger), Johann Burger, Ladislaus Suntheim, Stephanus Rosinus, Henricus Eutycus. Eubolius, Polymnius, Burger, and Rosinus were professors at the University. Rosinus had been Celtis' pupil at Ingolstadt and became a professor of mathematics at Vienna as well as court chaplain, canon at St. Stephen's and elsewhere. Suntheim gained some prominence as court chaplain and historian engaged in work on Maximilian's genealogy. Heinrich Euticus the younger followed his teacher from Ingolstadt to Vienna in 1499. Other humanists of varying degrees of prominence joined the sodality. The list of members could be expanded indefinitely, if all those participating in humanist activities were to be included.

After the death of Celtis the sodality was perpetuated by one of his students, Georg Tannstetter (Collimitius) who had come to Vienna in 1503 as professor of mathematics and astronomy at the University. The sodality came to be known as the *Sodalitas Collimitiana*. It lasted until 1521, but faded gradually into obscurity, though Collimitius lived until 1535.

Celtis was more of an agitator than an organizer. He began many more projects than he completed. His role in founding the learned sodalities provides a good example of his initial energy but lack of systematic perseverance. Celtis, first of all, envisioned the organization of four great literary sodalities for the four regions of Germany—the Rhenana, Danubiana, Vistulana, and Codonea (Baltica)—a scheme which figures in the *Amores*, in which each of his loves symbolizes the four points of the compass. Later Celtis conceived of a plan for a sevenfold sodality. In 1500, at any rate, he published with the short poems of Ausonius a poem to the seven sodalities, "Septenaria sodalitas litteraria Germanie." [1] It was characteristic of his imaginative flair and of his interest in geography that he named his proposed societies after the river, forest, or city where they would gather. In 1501 the edition of the works of Roswitha was published "sub priuilegio sodalitatis Celticae," containing the epigrams of the Literary Sodality of Germany. Dalberg's two contributions bear the superscription: "Joannes Dalburgius, Vormatiensis Episcopus, sodalitatis litterariae per universam Germaniam princeps." Vitez had died in 1499 and was not formally replaced as the head of the Sodalitas Danubiana. Dalberg alone remained as head of an existing sodality. The epigrams came from members both of the Rhenana and Danubiana. It was only natural that Dalberg should be honored as the prince of the one great sodality. Celtis was obviously here indulging in rhetoric in referring to a sodality of all Germany. There is no reason for supposing that such a society existed in reality.

Although the superstructure of large sodalities was never completed, the idea itself caught on. Sodalities sprang up in many cities on the local level, generally as smaller congregations of members of the two large sodalities, but here and there with no direct connection with Celtis' societies. The court people at Linz, where Maximilian frequently resided, named themselves the *Sodalitas litteraria Linciana.* The adult pupils of the Poets College which Celtis founded in Vienna were known as the *Sodales conscripti* of the *Sodalitas litteraria Collegii Viennensis.* At Ingolstadt, where Celtis had first given expression to his idea of founding an academy, his pupil Aventine, who was to gain fame as a Bavarian historian, with the cooperation of Prince Ernst, founded in 1516 the *Sodalitas litteraria Angilostadensis* or *Sodalitas litteraria Bojorum.* In 1501 Celtis' Leipzig friend, Martin Polich, or Mellerstadt, wrote a passage which indicates that he knew of the Sodalitas Rhenana, the Sodalitas Danubiana, and also a Sodalitas Leucopolitana apparently at Leipzig.

The imperial city of Augsburg with its rich burghers, lawyers, doctors, and the cathedral very naturally attracted its quota of humanists. The home of Conrad Peutinger, the city secretary, on the cathedral square became the center of humanist activities. Under his leadership the *Sodalitas litteraria Augustana* was founded sometime before 1503. Like the others it was loosely associated as a kind of local chapter of the Sodalitas Danubiana. Peutinger himself inscribed with his own hand the names of the members after the inscriptions in his work *Romanae vetustatis fragmenta*. In line with Peutinger's own interests, the chief concerns of the Augsburg Sodality were historical.

One of the most interesting of Celtis' Greek colonies was the *Sodalitas Maiorhoviana*, or *Marcomannica*, in Olmütz, a small town in Moravia, so named presumably after the meeting place, the Meierhof.[2] One of the members wrote of a *Lex sodalitatis*, but it is doubtful whether this sodality was any better organized than the others. Celtis was the happy recipient of a constant stream of gifts from these small-town admirers as well as from the other comrades—plums, wine, rabbits, beaver, fur, books, and maps. The greatest event for the Sodalitas Maiorhoviana was the visit Celtis paid to Olmütz in August 1504. He came to arrange details for the contribution of the sodality to his proposed *Germania illustrata*, a historico-geographical description of Moravia.

Elsewhere in the Empire similar sodalities arose, at least some of them inspired by the precedent set by Celtis. His Ingolstadt successor, Jakob Locher, Philomusus, called a similar group after himself, the *Philomusea Sodalitas*. Wimpheling called into being the *Strassburg Literary Sodality*. Mutianus Rufus in Gotha gathered a similar coterie of humanist friends in the sanctuary of *Beata Tranquilitas*. And, although there were sufficient Italian examples to follow, also Aldus Manutius' plans for a "Neacademy" of learned men to serve the cause of scholarship in Venice may have been given added momentum by the enthusiasm and activism of Celtis. They corresponded and Celtis planned several times, in 1497, for example, in 1498, and again in 1501, to visit Venice. Aldus planned, in fact, to found the Academy in Germany, probably in Vienna, if Maximilian would provide the proper support.[3]

Besides such standard humanist preoccupations as the searching for codices, copying inscriptions, collecting antiquities, and the like, the most important function of the sodality was, Celtis believed, to publish the classic authors and contemporary humanist writings, especially his own. It was their usual procedure to exchange manuscripts for criticism before delivering them to the printer. Neither Celtis nor the great majority of his colleagues could in any real sense be considered scholars. They were men of action, publicists, enthusiasts, poets, but not men of erudition. A survey of the membership of the sodalities makes very clear that the humanists and proselytes of the gate in Celtis' great company were by and large men engaged in the active life. Doctors and lawyers predominated, most of them academicians, though a good number attached to princely, royal, or the imperial court, some holding high office. Some were well to do burghers in the prosperous free imperial cities. Only the Olmütz group in its quiet provincial way was dominated by schoolmasters. And in all churchmen—canons, prebend holders, monks, abbots, and bishops—made up a good part of the membership. Neither socially nor intellectually did the sodalities have any fundamental quarrel to make with the established order.

What was new was the devotion to the new learning. The cause of the *ars humanitatis*, of poetic culture, was the common denominator commanding the attention and loyalty of these men of varying professions and callings. It is true that the triple palimpsest of Latin, Greek, and Hebrew writings contained revolutionary ingredients. They brought novel or renewed ideas about literature, patriotism, and philosophy. But the northern humanists read them still in the main from the old parchment. It may not, however, be too remote a comparison to see in the sodalities the forerunners of the patriotic Klopstock's republic of learned men who should marshal the spiritual forces of the land. When in 1512 on the eve of the Reuchlin controversy which shook the world of humanism, Beatus Rhenanus named the humanists who under the leadership of his idol Erasmus were the ornaments of Germany, almost half their number were alumni of Celtis' sodalities.

# In Maximilian's Vienna

CELTIS exulted because the call to Vienna meant that he "could at last bring in his uncertain and straying ship and drop anchor in a tranquil port." Having pursued the study of eloquence and philosophy with long and difficult peregrinations in the manner of Plato and Pythagoras, he would now contribute to the increase of learning at the University and to the erudition of the German youth. The decade of wandering since his crowning as poet laureate was followed by ten years in Vienna, the last years of his life.

He could hardly have found a more propitious vantage point for furthering his humanist ideals than Maximilian's Vienna. The humanists hailed the advent of Maximilian to the throne for they anticipated an era of new prosperity under this friend of learning. Nor were they disappointed. With the accession of Maximilian, all the Habsburg dynastic holdings were united in one hand for the first time in one hundred and twenty-five years. It was only natural that he should envision himself as the restorer of the ancient imperial dignity. He shines in tradition as the last of the knights. A man of action, though, as Machiavelli observed, of inconsistent designs, he captivated the imagination of the people. Seldom had a Habsburg been so popular.

The hearts of the humanists, too, were his. Trithemius wrote: "There is no one in Germany possessed of a greater intellectual curiosity, a more sincere love for manifold studies and the true joy in the prospering of the sciences and arts than King Maximilian." He favored the humanists but used them for his purposes. They could be useful in molding public opinion. That he did them the service of drawing them from the shelter of the schools into the arena of world affairs was for their good but not entirely to his credit. Celtis, called to Vienna by Maximilian's regents, devoted himself directly or indirectly to his service thereafter. He was the man chosen to represent the humanist studies at the university at the very time when the superintendent Perger was promoting reform with renewed enthusiasm. In 1499 the regents themselves stepped in and threw the weight of their authority behind reform. On August 8, 1499, the arts faculty expressed its thanks to the Emperor for establishing lectures in the humanities. Celtis was by no means a pioneer of humanism at Vienna. There was a tradition of at least half a century of interest in classic studies. His appointment could hardly be called an unprecedented innovation.

Celtis maintained a very independent position in relation to the arts faculty. He had been called by the emperor over the opposition of the superintendent and felt, therefore, that he had special prerogatives. He did not, for example, register in the matriculation book, as he should have, until the winter semester of 1507/1508, when he was at last enrolled as a member of the Rhenish nation. He chose his lecture hours without consideration for the official regulations. A friend sent him a letter from Elysium, signed Caius Plinius, urging him to actualize his humanist program and to begin once more his discontinued lectures. The move to a new school had obviously not altered some of his less commendable habits. This kind of conduct coupled with his comments about the sophists and hooded monks, the university church being served by the Dominicans,

was quite enough to stimulate sharp criticism and even controversy. A friend wrote him from far-off Rostock:

I understand, most beloved Celtis, that you in these days now
past have stood in the greatest peril of losing your good name. For
since "fame is not swifter than any evil," here in the farthest corner
of Germany it has been reported that you have published a certain
book [presumably Apuleius] in which you have worshiped, venerated, and adored Phoebus, Mercury, and Apollo as if you despised our saints and God like a gentile and this has been preached
publicly by certain religious men in the University of Vienna. But
now, as I hear, you have in the presence of the regents so refuted
the religious and certain antiquarians of the University of Vienna,
dialecticians and Alexandrine philosophers, that you covered over
the mouths of all those and their defamation against the poets.
And in the same measure as they at first persecuted you in hatred,
they now love and admire you.

The friend goes on to deplore the ignorance of literature and
the inertia of the monks and relates various anecdotes illus-
trating the jealousies between the Dominicans and the Min-
orites and other monkish quarrels.[1] It is an instructive incident
and the analysis implied in the letter is probably basically correct. There was a not unwarranted resentment against the free
substitution of pagan for Christian names by the poets. Moreover, the rivalries between the orders and now between the
traditionalists and the innovators were an old and not very
elevating story. But there is no indication here of a basic conflict of two systems of thought, of scholasticism as a meta-
physical discipline and humanism as a new world view. Rather,
the differences between Celtis and his detractors seem to have
been rather easily resolved. What is more, this was really the
only time that the frictions in the faculty came to the surface.
There is almost no other evidence that Celtis experienced any
difficulty at Vienna.

He lectured, as at Ingolstadt, on the standard humanist

topics, Ciceronian rhetoric, the odes of Horace, grammar, rhetoric, and poetry. He showed freshness and originality in his teaching, publishing a number of works with wide margins so that the students would be able to write notes upon his lectures next to the text. The first of these remarkable publications was the cosmography of Lucius Apuleius, *De Mundo*, which he published immediately on his arrival in Vienna and dedicated to Krachenberger and Fuchsmagen out of gratitude for their intervention in behalf of his call.[2]

This was to be viewed as a test edition, "a little morsel such as the merchants offer prospective customers so that they might be drawn as by an appetizing drink to the mysteries which are handled in philosophy and the divine poetry." From it could be learned the process of the creation of the world-all, how it was framed and exists as a whole and in its parts, "according to the number and order of that Creator and Father of all things with the highest wisdom and wonderful beauty." Things divine and human are bound inseparably together. To contemplate on it in this short life is a worthy occupation for in so doing the spirit is raised from its bonds into the divine and heavenly realms and has a taste of eternal salvation. It shares in the tables of the gods with the nectar and ambrosia of Jupiter.

Celtis' interest in geography of a scientifically questionable sort was evidenced again the next year, 1498. He planned to have a student edition of Ptolemy's *Cosmography* published in Venice. But illness prevented the trip and the plan was never realized. An edition of Juvenal which he considered earlier failed to materialize. Celtis was so much the enthusiast and aesthete, so little the scholar and thinker.

Easily the most important of the publications intended to serve as a basis for his university lectures and the inspiration of the members of the sodalities was Cornelius Tacitus' *Germania*. This Celtis published in 1500, together with a poetic work of his own, the *Germania generalis*, dedicated to Maximilian, which was to serve as a preliminary sample of the greater work to follow, the *Germania illustrata*.³ It had been one of the major finds of the humanists' own exciting age of discovery. The *Germania* provided a new rosy dawn for German history.⁴ It was not, therefore, its originality or any inherent excellence in Celtis' Tacitus edition which gave it considerable significance, but the fact that he produced it as a publicist at a time when patriotic feeling was building up in the Empire as never before. Celtis was the first humanist to lecture on Tacitus in a German university.

Something of a patriotic motive may have influenced his selection of the *De Li Non Aliud* of Nicolas Cusanus for lectures and publication, for here was one of the greatest German philosophers of the century. Doubtless the intriguing form of the *De Li Non Aliud*, a series of twenty antithetical propositions, attracted the dilettante philosopher and made him select this minor piece of Cusanus above others of greater substance. With it Celtis included a sapphic ode in the manner of Horace, the "Carmen saeculare" commemorating the end of one century and beginning of the new. Celtis was most hopeful that the new century would bring Germany to a new greatness.

Three other minor works dating from around 1500 may be considered part of this genre of Celtis' publications. The first of these was the *Oeconomia*, a collection of charming epigraphs on the household of a philosopher. The second of these smaller publications was a combination of four small pieces. The booklet began merely, "In hoc libello continentur . . ." It contained, besides the poem of Celtis to the seven literary sodalities, two selections from the fourth-century poet Ausonius playing again upon the number seven, the seven wise men, and the famous letter of St. Jerome to Magnus a Roman orator. In it Jerome explained why he considered secular literature of value also in the service of Christian truth. This was the same letter that Erasmus cited in the *Antibarbari* to the same end. Jerome was truly the patron saint of the northern humanists. Finally, Celtis republished the ode on what a young philosopher should know as an exhortation also to his Vienna students, "Protrepticus ingeniorum puerorum."[5] In not a single work which he edited did Celtis make any textual emendations, improvements, or correction. Critical scholarship was not his forte.

Celtis worked hard to promote the study of Greek at Vienna, and was himself the first man to interpret Homer in a German university. He tried to bring a regular professor of Greek to the University; but, in spite of his efforts, a regular professorship was not established until 1523.[6]

Celtis' relations with the arts faculty seems to have been reasonably satisfactory. He continued to bait the scholastics, at least when among his friends, but there was much less friction than there had been at Ingolstadt. When he conceived the idea of founding a separate college for poets and mathematicians, it was due, less to university opposition to his program than to his desire for a more effective instrument for promoting humanist learning than that afforded by a mere professorship. The type of academy which he had first visualized at Ingolstadt for promoting the aims of his Inaugural Address was not the same as the sodalities now organized. He had in mind, rather, an institute for instruction where with able colleagues he could promote his program among the students. In planning for the new Poets College, Celtis was forging an instrument, not for battle with the arts faculty, but to help carry the day in a much larger field.

In the spring of 1501 Celtis had an opportunity to present his plan to the Emperor and his officials directly, at Bolzano in the South Tyrol. The Emperor was convinced. On October

31, 1501, he issued at Celtis' expense the charter which called the Poets College into being. There should be two professors in poetry and oratory and two professors erudite in mathematics. The first instructor in poetry should be the head of the college and superintendent of the lectures. Moreover, for the increased honor and prestige of the University, by imperial authority, the privilege and prerogative should be granted to the college of crowning with the laurel anyone who had studied oratory and poetry in the University and had been diligently examined by the said Poets College. Conrad Celtis, the *lector ordinarius* in poetry and oratory at the University, and his successors as head of the college should grant the privileges thereunto appertaining, though the act of bestowing the laurel wreath should be reserved for the Emperor himself. Throughout the charter the close integration of the college with the University is emphasized.

Celtis had already taken steps for housing the new college. He had a gift for providing for his domestic comfort. At first upon his arrival in Vienna he had stayed with some jurists. Then he moved into a house belonging to the medical faculty. In July 1500, he was already negotiating with the abbot of the Cistercian monastery at Neuberg an der Mürz in Styria for renting the Neubergerhof by St. Ann's, a house of imposing size standing at Grünangergasse 1, two blocks from St. Stephen's, near the old university building. At first he occupied three rooms; then, in order to accommodate the Poets College, the whole house. The rent was paid by the vice-chancellor of Austria. He gathered there a library of humanist books, and globes and maps of heaven and earth.

During the winter months Celtis was busy organizing. On his forty-third birthday, February 1, 1502, he celebrated with his friends the festive inauguration of the Poets College. Vinzenz Lang (Longinus), whom Celtis chose as his colleague, delivered a stirring panegyric to Maximilian for his services to learning which was published that year with the *Amores*. Andreas Stiborius was appointed to one of the two chairs of mathematics. The college demonstrated the constructive relationship that might have been between humanism and science.

Behind the text of his play, *Rhapsodia*, Celtis published a list of the three classes of the college, four students in each, with a poem by each celebrating Maximilian's services to the Muses. But Celtis' hope that these twelve men would lift poetic culture to new heights was never realized. None really gained any literary reputation. The Poets College itself came to an early end. The presentation of the *Rhapsodia* in 1504 seems to have been the apogee of its short life. In that year, however, Longinus died and was not replaced. With failing health Celtis carried on alone. In his testament he did not even mention the College, referring to himself merely as a *lector ordinarius* of poetry at Vienna. It would seem that the College had preceded its founder into the land of shadows. Celtis, indeed, lacked the talent and temperament of a college dean.

If Celtis' formal activities as an educator left much to be desired, he was none the less an inspiration to his students. Some of them became men of real stature. Aventine, who became the noted historian of Bavaria, followed him from Ingolstadt to Vienna where he lived in his house and was in the closest personal relationship to him. Cuspinian, the historian of the Habsburgs and of Austria, called Celtis the "great hope of Germany." Jakob Ziegler, one of the founders of historical geography and a reformer of the Erasmian type, praised him highly for his services to arts and letters and owed to him much of his interest in nature. From St. Gallen in 1501/1502 came Joachim von Watt, or Vadianus, one of Celtis' prize students, destined to become the Reformer of his native city.

Both the stalwart opponent of Luther, Dr. Eck, and the

Swiss reformer, Zwingli, came to Celtis for classic learning. Zwingli enrolled at Vienna in 1498, was apparently expelled for some reason, as the striking of his name in the matriculation book and the marginal notation "exclusus" indicates, but re-registered in 1500.[7] There is little information on their contacts, though Zwingli's spiritualized view of nature and somewhat syncretistic view of religion give a hint of the direction of his influence. It is interesting to suppose that, when Luther quite rightly confronted Zwingli with the charge, "You are of a different spirit," he discerned a mind not untouched by the ideas of the Vienna humanist.

# Playwright

E VEN THOUGH the humanists were primarily lyricists and rhetoricians rather than dramatists, it was from their work that the new form of modern drama developed. Celtis, too, made his contribution. He believed that drama could be used as a rhetorical means to effect a moral and patriotic end. In "Ingolstadt Address" he described the value of drama and urged the imitation of the ancients:

It was truly a great and almost divine factor in the administration of their state that they were eager to unite wisdom with eloquence and in order to achieve this end established public performances in which with sublime persuasion and remarkable inventiveness they exhorted the spectators to virtue, piety, moderation, courage, and the patient endurance of all hardships. They warned the youth against vices and encited them to seek glory so that what they owed the fatherland, their friends, their hosts, and their dear parents, they imbibed as though from living pictures.

Such an enthusiasm for the theater could have only one source. This, too, Celtis had learned from the Italians.

Since the end of the fourteenth century the Italian humanists had already been composing dramatic works of their own. Terence and Plautus were the most popular classic models for these productions. The first German attempts at classic comedy took place among the student circles in the Italian universities. The first school edition of Terence in Germany was published in Strassburg in 1470. But the extensive use of Terence and Plautus began in the 1490's and continued throughout the next century. When Luther entered the monastery, he had a copy of each under his arm. The most notable early attempts at writing original dramas were made by men of Celtis' humanist circle. But he himself was by no means the first to produce one.

The credit for the first original drama must be given Jakob Wimpheling for his *Stylpho* written in 1480. With it he bridged the way from the tradition of rhetorical declamation to dramatic action. A much more notable effort was Johannes Reuchlin's *Henno* which his students performed on January 31, 1497, in Dalberg's house for the Heidelberg Sodality. Reuchlin had already written one comedy, *Sergius*, against Holzinger, the chancellor of Duke Eberhard the younger. Dalberg advised against its performance. Celtis regarded Reuchlin highly as the founder of humanist comedy.

At last in Vienna Celtis had the necessary leisure and talent to establish public performances like the ancients. He selected the same two dramas as had his Cracow student, Laurentius Corvinus, now at St. Elizabeth School in Breslau—the *Eunuchus* of Terence and the *Aulularia* of Plautus—and presented them in the winter semester of 1502/1503 in the "aula" or assembly hall of the University. He posted notices of the performances which are the oldest theater bills in Vienna:

For the comedy of Eunuchus acted out in Latin:

> Who desires to see an old Roman play
> As it was produced on a stage in the Roman Forum
> Let him hasten, when shining Phoebus shows the first hour,
> To the beautiful hall of the university.

On the dramatization of Aulularia in the hall of Vienna:

> Who desires to see a genuine Latin play
> As they were often seen in the schools of Rome
> And as they were once performed in the theater
>     of learned Hellas,
> While the audience clapped its hands in approval,
> Let him come as a spectator in the assembly hall,
> When the hammer of the clock first strikes one.[1]

The plays were probably acted out on a podium, since the humanists made the transition from the medieval stage to the elevated modern stage. The assembly hall was well decorated for the event, for Celtis had supplied verses to accompany wall paintings of the Emperor, the threefold platonic philosophy, and himself.

The performance of the plays was well received. Celtis' friend Wilhelm Pülinger, Polymnius, a member of the sodality, as rector of the University in the winter semester, 1502/1503, wrote in the Acts of the University: "It was indeed a memorable presentation such as I and others had never before seen. A number of comedies were presented with my permission in the assembly hall of the university, produced by students in a theatrical setting in the view of many observers."

The drama naturally attracted Celtis, for it had all the elements of display, festivity, and comradery at which he excelled. On March 1, 1501, he and some members of the Danubian Sodality presented his first drama, the *Ludus Dianae*, before the court of Maximilian and his Italian bride, Bianca Maria Sforza, in Linz. Peter Bonomus, Josef Grünpeck, Celtis, Dietrich Ulsenius, and Vinzenz Lang played the part of the leading mythological characters. Lang was Bacchus, Ulsenius, judging from his carefree character, was probably Silenus. Celtis was perhaps Silvanus, since the elaborate acrostics in the speech of Silvanus was a special point of pride with him. The Italian Bonomus may have played Diana and Grünpeck perhaps introduced the drama as Mercury the herald.

The *Ludus Dianae* followed the Italian pattern in the free use of classic forms and figures in the manner of the festival plays using both rhetorical declamation and pantomime. It had many features in common with the "Fastnachtspiele" and so combined elements both of the older folk tradition and the newer masque comedy. It was not difficult to choose a theme, for Diana, the goddess of the hunt, was sure to appeal to the Emperor. Celtis was at a loss to name his work, so he called it a "play of Diana in the manner of a comedy."[2]

Like Seneca, Celtis divided his play into five acts, with a prologue preceding it. Unlike the classic dramas, there was no dialogue, no suspense or real drama. Each act merely represented a picture in which the leading figures declaimed their pieces. In the prologue, Mercury enters to announce the advent of Diana. In the first act the horned Diana appears with a company of nymphs, satyrs, and fauns to present their bows, quivers, and spears to the king, the mighty hunter. Diana praises the Emperor as the keenest and most persistent man of the chase and symbolically makes him the ruler of all hunters. The act closes with the whole troupe singing in four voices the chorus of praise to Maximilian and Bianca Maria while the nymphs dance in a circle about them. In the second act Silvanus enters, accompanied by Bacchus, the fauns, and satyrs. The god of the woods praises Maximilian as the lord of war. He urges him to attack the faithless crowds of unbelieving and pursue the fierce spirit of the fearful demon Mohammed, a theme familiar to the Emperor from his Burgundian days and an old song to Celtis, who had urged the same on Frederick with the same result. He hopes that he will be able to check the Venetians, French, and the Swiss. After his address the whole company dances and joins in the chorus of praises in four voices accompanied by a fife and zither. In the printed version Celtis could not refrain from adding a few lines calling attention to the artistic arrangements of his poem which had not been equaled for a long time. The climax comes in the third act with the festive crowning of Vinzenz Lang, playing the role of Bacchus. Bacchus arrives with his perpetually drunken comrade, Silenus, and a host of devotees. He delivers an oration relating his long journey from hot India to the Greeks and Romans and the banks of the Rhine and praising the wonders of German wine, especially in Vienna, where the fertile Kahlenberg bows his vine-covered head to the swollen Danube. Then, prostrating himself at the feet of the Emperor, he implores Maximilian to place upon his head the laurel wreath. At this point the Emperor enters the play, bestowing on Longinus the requested laurel, a unique touch of audience participation. The whole chorus thereupon joins in a three-part ode of thanks to the Emperor. The brief fourth act, in a scene reminiscent of Rubens' painting, "The Drunken Silen," provides still more comic relief as Silenus rides in upon an ass holding a tumbler in his hand and complaining about his long ears. On his request the Emperor permits wine to be poured into golden beakers while kettledrums and horns sound out. In the final act all the players assemble and Diana thanks the Emperor and his bride, wishes them many heirs, and bids them farewell. The chorus repeats her speech singing in four voices.

The players were not without their reward, for the next day the Emperor invited all twenty-four to a royal banquet and bestowed generous gifts on them. Celtis added two verses to the *Ludus Dianae* when he published it on May 13 in Nuremberg, thanking him again for his gifts and services to the muses and making an aside at the barbarous monks and their stinking cowls. Maximilian, the warrior, gave him an occasion for his next foray into the theater world.

The Bavarian War of Succession was raging in 1504. On September 12, Maximilian fell upon a troop of Bohemian auxiliaries on their way to join the Palatinate forces at Wenzenbach near Regensburg and defeated them completely. The Bohemians ever since the Hussite wars had rivaled the Swiss in reputation as fighters. But there was really no occasion for glory, for Maximilian had every advantage including an overwhelming numerical superiority. Celtis seized the opportunity to celebrate Maximilian's victory in a public play presented by the students in his Poets College. He presented the *Rhapsodia* in Vienna. It was less of a drama even than the *Ludus Dianae*, more a piece of declamatory rhetoric.

In the *Rhapsodia* the Emperor and the seven electors are seated on the stage. Paresiphanus, as the first speaker, praises the honored guests. Then follows Heroldus, the proclaimer, who urges the youth to praise Maximilian who, by his victory over the Bohemians, has established eternal peace. Paresiphanus now calls on Phoebus and the Muses to celebrate the great imperial triumph. Phoebus reiterates the summons to the Muses. Mercury appears with Phoebus announcing his participation in the festival, since he had brought that wrong counsel which had led the unthinking people to their ruin. Bacchus, accompanied by satyrs and fauns, promises to dance around the Muses and with his beakers inspire artistic verses. Thereupon each of the Muses in turn, beginning with Clio, step forward and praise the Emperor extravagantly. Terpsichore compares Maximilian with Greek and Roman conquerors. Calliope lauds him as greater than Charlemagne, the Ottos, and even Frederick Barbarossa. Urania calls for the defeat of the Turks and the Bohemian heretics. Thereupon a poet who wishes to be crowned comes before the throne. He expresses a twofold wish: for the freeing of Constantinople and for the laurel crown—wishes which Celtis seems to equate in importance.

The one is within the power of the Emperor, who crowns the poet. The Muses dance around Apollo standing with zither in hand wishing the Emperor victory and trophies everywhere. Bacchus and the satyrs enter dancing and singing a song for the defeat of the perfidious Turks and the expulsion of the Poles, Swedes, and Bohemians from the land. Mercury then commends the Muses to the Emperor who responds, "No one of those here present shall go unrewarded, defending here and everywhere your chorus." Mercury at last bids the spectators farewell and asks also their favor for the Muses.

Celtis published the *Rhapsodia* the following year in Augsburg. The *Rhapsodia* was presented by the students of the Poets College.[3] It is clear from the list of participants that they represented the upper social classes, sons of high officials, city patricians, and even nobles. Celtis was not without diplomatic skill and not above playing favorites. The poet crowned in the play by a student or perhaps by Celtis himself was Sigismund Fuchsmagen, the orator, a son of the regent Johannes.

In order to tone down the offensiveness of his *Ludus* to his friends in Bohemia, who, like Augustinus Moravus, were incensed that he should celebrate such a battle of frogs and mice in which cavalry had defeated infantry with overwhelming numbers, he included with the play some selections designed to suggest that he exulted in the defeat only of heretical Bohemians. He published with the *Rhapsodia* also the poems of praise to Maximilian composed by twelve students of the Poets College in gratitude for its founding. Celtis had sent them to Aldus in Venice, but he declined to publish them for fear of the French, quoting Ovid, "For do you not know that kings have long arms?"

Celtis wrote also a third *Ludus* which has not as yet been rediscovered. It was apparently presented before the court of

Maximilian on February 2, 1506, when he visited Vienna and was greeted with an address by Cuspinian. Judging from a woodcut by Burgkmair which presumably served as the frontispiece to this drama, it was an allegory on the disciplines cultivated at the Poets College and the University under Maximilian's protection. The mystical number seven recurs in the seven days of creation, the seven mechanical arts of man, the seven liberal arts, and the Muses. Philosophy, however, supplies the highest wisdom. The temptations which draw the students away from the best disciplines is typified by the Judgment of Paris. Pallas is victorious and the reward is the laurel wreath which assures eternal fame. If the association of this woodcut with the drama is valid, it is clear that this third drama was also in the nature of a rhetorical allegory.[4]

Celtis' dramas were in no real sense dramatic. They contained elements both of the traditional *Fastnachtspiel* and of the newer Italian courtly masque comedies. It was typical of the *Fastnachtspiel*, for example, to have heralds announce the play. They still appear in Hans Sachs. The Judgment of Paris theme was also common. Celtis' plays were reminiscent of such Italian court productions as Politian's *Orpheus*, one of the earliest of this type. That he had learned little from classic drama bears repetition.[5] The frieze of the recently renovated "Goldenes Dachl" in Innsbruck shows Maximilian and his two wives intently watching a court play. Mary of Burgundy and Bianca of Milan symbolize the variant influences on Celtis' drama, that of the North and that of the South.

The work of Celtis and the humanists had in turn an influence on the school dramas of the Reformation period and later on the pageantry, opera, and drama of the Baroque, when the whole court took part in the presentation. The *Ludi Caesari* of the Jesuits were also designed for festival occasions. This development was foreshadowed by a play performed in the Scottish monastery in Vienna in 1515. There Benedictus Chelidonius had his students present, in the manner of Celtis, a play on the battle of lust and virtue. In the audience were the Cardinal Matthäus Lang, Maria, the future queen of Hungary, and playing a part was the young prince later to become Emperor, Charles V.

Celtis would have considered his odes and dramas incomplete without musical accompaniment. "Phoebus, come thou and place upon my brow the sacred laurel, so that with the sound of the pleasant lyre, I may unite my sweet songs" (*Oeconomia*). He himself played a number of stringed instruments, the lute, the violin, and zither. He was interested also in the organ, though he could not play it. He did know and inspired some of the great organists of Maximilian's court, however. In Cracow he associated with Heinrich Finck, the first German master of the grand style. Finck lived the life of the wandering artists, eventually ending his days in Vienna. Celtis associated also with the greatest organist of the period, Paul Hofhaimer, one of the leading musicians of Maximilian's court chapel circle and organist of St. Stephen's in Vienna. Other musicians, too, came within the orbit of his radiant inspiration—Michael, Senfl, and Tritonius.

The *Ludus Dianae* was accompanied by music. The notes for the chorus were printed with the Nuremberg edition of 1501. Celtis was himself the "discoverer" of the German humanist ode widely used during the sixteenth century. The music of the *Ludus Dianae* was the first outstanding humanist ode with all its major characteristics. The typical music of the Renaissance was the *musica reservata* which spread from Italy. It was a type based on the word, following the effective content of the text. The representative form of this type was the madrigal. The German humanist ode descended from this form, but, instead of expressing the content of the text, it merely effected the tonation of the metrical scheme. The Italians followed an aesthetic goal, the Germans more a scholarly philological interest. The humanists were absolutely convinced that the classic lyrics were sung, not spoken. Since classic music had not survived, they undertook to reproduce it. In Italy the songs between the acts of dramas were set to music and when the dialogue, too, was set to music, the opera had arrived. This was first done in 1594 in Jacopo Peri's *Dafne*.

The Italian Frottole already contained the basic elements of the humanist ode. Reuchlin had set the choruses of his *Henno* to simple one-voice melodies. Celtis felt that Latin verse knew no accental tonation, but, in both speaking and singing was expressed only by longs and shorts. He had Horace's odes set to music constructed on this principle and at the close of his lecture he had the students sing them to reëmphasize the scansion. And though he seems to have borrowed the melody for the choruses of the *Ludus Dianae* from the Italian Franciscus Niger, the addition of multiple voices was perhaps his own. But that he composed them himself is open to serious question.[6]

The composer with whom Celtis worked most closely was Petrus Tritonius (Treybenreif) from Bozen in the South Tyrol. Tritonius, already well along in years, enrolled at Ingolstadt on February 28, 1497, where he studied under Celtis. He seems later to have followed him to Vienna. There he completed the composition of melodies for a collection of odes by Horace and Celtis—the *Melopoiae* which he published under the auspices of Celtis and the literary sodality in 1507 in Augsburg.[7] Others followed this lead, such as Cochlaeus in his *Tetrachordon Musices*, Senfl, and Hofhaimer. This style of the humanist ode did have some influence on the harmony of voices in the evangelical church hymn. Tritonius' last work, in fact, was the publication of one hundred and thirty-one old church hymns with the notes written in by hand. Celtis was highly pleased with the humanist achievements. Poetry and music were closely allied, for was not the *carmen* of the poet derived from the *canere* of the musician? He had earlier modestly conceded:

> *We dance, we sing, we paint not badly*
> *And smoothly we play the resonant chords.*[8]

# Poet

CELTIS was first and foremost a poet. "Oh sacred and mighty work of the poets, you alone free all things from fate and lift up mortal ashes to the stars!"[1] His ambition was to be remembered among the Germans as Horace was in Italy. He was a good lyric poet, the best, in fact, that German humanism produced. The poet was to him more than a master of good letters and a rhymer. He was fond of the term *vates* in speaking of the poet, a name, restored to favor by Virgil, which carried the connotation of the *poeta* as a prophet, a sage, an authority, yes, a philosopher. The true poet had a divine genius which led his spirit to strive heavenward. To him the office of the poet was a calling. With the Renaissance emphasis on the autonomy of the aesthetic realm, the poet's position was no longer considered inferior to that of the philosopher. Imagination or inspiration was the special gift of the poet and a legitimate avenue to essential truth.

Celtis was not too devoted to his theories of the divine madness of the poet to forget the realities of the poet's craft. He knew that the poet's genius could sour at times. The poet had to dig like a soldier and plow like a peasant to bring his verse in order. The oracle of Apollo pronounced to him: "Great fame comes to no one without great labor and widespread glory always requires perspiration."[2] Celtis was too little disciplined to complete all of his projects. Of his three main works, the *Amores*, the *Odes*, and the *Epigrams*, he brought only the first to the publisher himself and he had to be coaxed and cajoled to do so.

In March 1502, he traveled to Nuremberg to supervise an omnibus edition of his various works now ready for the press. On the way he was fallen upon and robbed by two brigands lying in wait in a heavily wooded pass. Except for the loss of his money he was none the worse for the adventure. As the year before when he published his *Roswitha*, he stayed in the home of the humanist patrician Wilibald Pirckheimer on the market place in the heart of the old city. Celtis called his house a "scriptorium or poet refuge." Through its door passed many famous guests, such as Regiomontanus, Hutten, Luther, and Melanchthon. Celtis remained on good terms with Pirckheimer, corresponded with him occasionally, and borrowed his books. Pirckheimer had the usual trouble with his loans and once wrote Celtis in good humor: "You write me that my Homer will come flying back to me, but I do not believe it. For if he had feathers of lead or were entirely lame, he would long since have returned to me."

The Pirckheimer family was most gifted, and Celtis' correspondence with Wilibald's sister, Charitas, a nun and, after 1503, abbess of the St. Clara convent in Nuremberg, is of great interest. The nuns of St. Clara came from the very best of Nuremberg families. Two sisters and two daughters of Wilibald represented the Pirckheimers. Erasmus said of them, "England had the daughters of More and Germany the Pirckheimer ladies." The exchange between the pure and sheltered nun and the coarse and worldly humanist symbolized two diverse tendencies of the age.

Celtis presented to Charitas a copy of Roswitha's dramas which he had published the year before. Her response was charming:

A few days ago I received the beloved writings of the learned virgin Roswitha which your lordship sent to me in my insufficiency without deserving it in the least. For this I rejoice that the Benefactor of the Soul grants deep wisdom not only to right thinking and learned men, but also does not deny to the weaker sex and the retarded creature a few crumbs which fall from the tables of the richly learned. The word of the apostle proved to be true in the case of that young virgin: "What the world thought weak God chose to shame the mighty." Praiseworthy indeed is the grace of the Holy Ghost who ornamented and decorated this virgin talent with such brilliance of knowledge and industry. Your care in publishing the writings and poems of a woman without despising the weaker sex and the humble position of a little nun is also to be praised and lauded. . . Forgive I ask the boldness which allowed me to address your honor with my maidenlike and uncultured letter. I blushed as I wrote this uncouth and unpolished letter. But I did it out of love for my beloved brother, who is very friendly disposed toward you. Whom he loves, I also love. May that charity which suffers all things pardon also my errors with good will.[3]

Celtis was quite taken. He composed an ode praising Charitas as an ornament of the Fatherland, his comfort in adversity. He presented it to her and with it the new edition of his *Amores*—an odd gift for a nun. Her answer was a classic example of the conservative religious reaction to the antique orientation of the poet:

I cannot in truth deny that the description and praise of the earthly fatherland in your book which pleased me very much would be even more congenial and delightful to me if it were a description and praise of the heavenly fatherland, Jerusalem above, from whence we come to this vale of misery, calamity, and ignorance and to which we ought to aspire with all our might. . .

I invite your honor to an earnest consideration of the divine law and the Holy Scriptures, as my particularly beloved lord and master, for whom I wish the highest regard in the eyes of God. Exactly for this reason I ask you not to delay this consideration. Now, most beloved, you must do what you can. You do not know when you will die and what awaits you after death is hidden from your eyes. Tomorrow is an unknown day and you do not know whether you will have a day after. Therefore, while you have time, gather for yourself imperishable treasures. For we have here no abiding city, but seek one to come. It is not revealed to us when we shall leave this lump of clay in nakedness, taking nothing with us except our virtues and our sins, for which we shall receive reward or punishment according to the earnest decision of the just judge, who will demand of us works and not words. . .

Therefore, out of our singular friendship I admonish your worship to abandon the evil fables of Diana, Venus, Jupiter, and of other damned pagans who are now burning in hell fire whose names and memory all true men who agree with the Christian profession must expunge, detest, and deliver to complete oblivion. Now make for yourself sacred friends of God whose works should be honored and imitated, so that, when you depart from this life, they will receive you into eternal habitations. . .[4]

Celtis anticipated similar criticism from other quarters and, in the dedication of the *Amores* to Emperor Maximilian, he made an elaborate apology for the eroticism of his poems. Celtis marshaled a whole battery of arguments to explain the candid revelations of the *Amores*, most of them familiar since Valla and Aeneas. His critics could take the threefold oath, but he subscribed to the Greek proverb, "The wise will love, the foolish will worry himself to death." He was in these books teaching the youth to avoid the frauds of wicked women, teaching modesty and temperance. Some things he wrote in allegories, he explained, in the manner of the loftiest philosophers. Even the moralist Seneca praised Epicurus. Serious matters become more palatable when mixed with levity.

The architectonic arrangement of the *Amores* reveals again the author's fascination with Pythagorean numerology.[5] Each of the four books is devoted to a lover in one of the four corners of Germany beginning in the east, passing like the sun to the south, then to the west, and finally to the frozen north. Each represents one time of the day, one season of the year and one age in the life of man. With each is associated one of the four tempers. The four books, in turn, follow quite closely the same organization. The first elegy of the first book states the theme and the last of the final book serves as an epilogue. One of the first elegies of each book describes the journey into the land of the beloved, introducing the season of the year. The heart of each book then is the love adventures. The final poem is descriptive picturing the course of the Vistula, the Danube, the Rhine, and a trip on the North Sea to the mysterious island of Thule. The woodcuts serving as a frontispiece to each of the four books suggest an even more elaborate construction, a promise not fulfilled in the text.

Celtis, like Ovid, seems to have been created for writing love poems. He knew all the joys and sorrows of sensual love. He was experienced in all the artful devices of womankind—deceitful tears, angry looks, feigned sobs, deceptive actions. The female heart is never constant; what it spurns it seeks and what it hates it desires. Often he is as obscene as Martial. His artistic ideal of feminine beauty was typical of the ruling taste of the time and similar to the stylized composite picture of the Italian Firenzuola, *Della bellezza delle donne.* The true beauty must be of slender build with long blonde hair, dark eyes and eyebrows, a small mouth with slightly swelling lips, the chin short, small feet, the hands long and white. The skin must be very white and soft, with red cheeks, and must be sufficiently translucent so that the veins are visible underneath. Traces of this stereotype appear in the portrayal of his heroines.

Of the four, Hasilina, the love of the first book, was the paramour of his Cracow days. Elsula, to whom he dedicated a number of odes as well as the second book of his *Amores*, was most likely his mistress and possibly his housekeeper in Regensburg. Like Aeneas, Celtis, too, had an Ursula. She seems to

have won his heart and a place in the third book during his so-
journ on the Rhine in 1495. Barbara Cimbrica was most certainly not of Lübeck. She seems less real than the other three.
She was perhaps an older woman and a passing fancy of his at
Nuremberg, judging from a few cryptic references by his
mischievous friend Ulsenius. The trip to the island of Thule
with Barbara was purely a poetic invention, a skillful one.
There was very little of the neoplatonic cosmic love of which
he had spoken in his preface. In his love poetry he owed most
to Ovid, but in the larger scheme of the work, Celtis showed
originality and creative imagination.

Richly decorated with eleven woodcuts, the *Amores* provided a link between the literary and artistic Renaissance, between Celtis and Dürer. Celtis himself made the specifications
for the woodcuts which are preserved in a copy by Hartmann
Schedel.[6] They were followed with some variations. Three of
the woodcuts were definitely from the workshop of Albrecht
Dürer, done according to his design, the second illustration
showing Celtis presenting his book to the Emperor, the third
showing the female figure of philosophy even bearing his
signature and varying considerably from Celtis' directions,
and the last done for Pirckheimer, picturing Apollo changing
Daphne into a laurel tree—with the arms of the Pirckheimers
and Rieters, his wife's family, displayed in the upper margin.
It was, in fact, through Pirckheimer that Celtis and Dürer became acquainted. Pirckheimer sent Dürer's greetings in one
letter to Celtis: "Turer te salutat."[7] These woodcuts were
made, to borrow Panofsky's phrase, under the master's limited
liability, mostly based on slight sketches only.

There is a strong probability, judging from artistic style
and some corroborative evidence that Dürer contributed to
the illustration also of other Celtis publications. The fact that
the picture of St. Sebaldus on the second publication of his

sapphic ode to the saint was in a less Gothic style than the first has led some to attribute it to Dürer. There is no further proof for it, however. There is somewhat more evidence that Dürer contributed the preparatory sketches, though not the actual working drawing for the pictures in Celtis' Roswitha edition of 1501, showing Celtis presenting the Roswitha comedies to Elector Frederick the Wise and Roswitha presenting her writings to Emperor Otto. The designs were probably executed by the so-called Benedict Master. One of the woodcuts in the Gunther Ligurinus, most of which were based on the illustrations in the *Amores*, shows evidence of Dürer's touch, the Apollo on Mount Parnassus. Dürer may, in fact, have paid Celtis a last and lasting tribute by painting him as his companion viewing the pseudo-calvary in his great painting "The Martyrdom of the Ten Thousand" which he did in 1507/ 1508 on commission from Celtis' patron, Frederick the Wise, for the Castle Church in Wittenberg.[8]

The other woodcuts of the *Amores* clearly originated in the workshop of the more conservative Michael Wohlgemut. The first was the title page, naming the four cities, rivers, regions, and ages of man. The fourth showed Celtis at his desk surrounded by a border of mythological figures. The fifth to the eighth served as title pages to each of the four books, without artistic value but symbolically very meaningful. The ninth, a double-page illustration, showed Nuremberg almost exactly as Wohlgemut had done in Schedel's *Weltchronik*. The tenth was of St. Sebaldus.

The *Amores* was a handsome publication and for the humanists a great literary triumph. They received it with an almost hysterical enthusiasm. It was a kind of best-seller, for the Latin reading public at any rate. Longinus wrote from Vienna: "One would need many hours to describe with what joy and with what great honor copies of your *Amores* are read by all and the name of Celtis cherished. All have asked me to greet you for them and have promised you gifts upon your return. . . Live happily, for you are dear to all and will be famous to the world to come."[9]

In 1513 Celtis' student, Thomas Resch, together with Vadian, sent his *Odes* to Matthias Schürer of Strassburg for publication.[10] The book of odes was organized on the pattern of Horace who had joined with his four books of odes exactly seventeen epodes and a *carmen saeculare*, as did Celtis, though Horace did not use the terms. Horace's real rise to fame in German humanism he owed to Celtis. The *Odes* are similar to the *Amores* in organization, and could almost be rearranged on the same plan. However, Barbara Cimbrica is missing from the fourth book, indicating that this book was left unfinished and was completed by the collection by the editors of miscellaneous odes. Like the last book of the *Amores*, these last odes are concerned more with the great questions of life, love, and knowledge. The odes cover a greater variety of topics than the elegies of the *Amores* and have a more specific application. Like Horace he dedicated a great many of them to friends. These gnomic odes have a clue to their theme included in the title. The tenor or mood of the poem is also frequently indicated, as though a hint as to the nature of the musical accompaniment. Like the *Amores*, a great many of the poems are purely erotic in nature. Celtis was the first love poet of German humanism. Other odes are political, though fewer than in Horace, some polemical or satirical pieces. The themes are primarily classic, the eulogy of learned men, the praise of cities, invitations to a festivity and the like. But there are also poems to the saints and the invocation of Mary. The epodes are more satirical and polemical. Occasionally Celtis borrows some flourishes directly from Horace, but the dynamic movement of his poems lifts him above the simple form of the classic ode.

Basically his poetry is still German poetry in the Latin language.

Celtis was even less fortunate with his *Epigrams* which were not published until almost four hundred years after his death.[11] Each book was to comprise one hundred epigrams, though the manuscript failed to achieve such symmetry. The epigram, as Celtis defined it in the *Ars Poetica*, should be saturated with gall and biting wit. In one epigram Celtis observes that some people find fault with his books because they fear they will find their name in them just as thieves fear the judge.[12] They were in genre essentially imitations of the epigrams of Persius, Juvenal, Ausonius, Prosper, and Martial, though independent in content. In addition to the satirical kind, he composed also a variety of other epigrams in the classic pattern, poems to household articles, to pets, to dead animals, an inheritance from Hellenism, epitaphs, and poems to saints and friends. The epigrams underscore one major weakness of the humanists. Most of the humanists lacked real humor. They mocked a great many things human and divine. They seldom laughed at themselves.

Basically Celtis was of a poetic nature. He knew that there were good and bad poets, dry and creative ones. He was very alert, very much alive. Much of his poetry shows the impact of real happenings. His poetry was more visual than auditory. He made some attempts at imitating the sound of a bombardment, the rustling of the wind in the trees, and the lowing of a distant cowherd, but he really excelled in his descriptive passages. His landscapes are well done and reflect a true love for nature. Like Petrarch he delighted in picturing his love in a beautiful natural setting with the wind playing with her golden hair, the flowers giving off sweet scent, and the brook murmuring softly. He was skilled at describing the new budding of spring. The sight of ruins evoked a romantic surge of emotions. One of his most classic pieces of nature description was the allegorical picture of the flooding of the Rhine.[13] The god of the sea calls an assembly of the river deities. The fountain nymphs hasten from their mossy hideaways to answer the call of Father Ocean. Their hair flutters in the south wind. They admire themselves in mirrors in the bright sunlight, shake the dew from their members, sing and test the strength of their arms to see whether they can weather the waves of the sea. Again in the later Renaissance form he compared the circle of stars moving around the earth with a Morisco dance about a celebrated beauty in the center quietly observing the wild performance. There are, on the other hand, much pedantry, many dull passages, and trite turns in his poetry.

Everywhere the poet himself is evident and his personality comes through. It is he himself which interests him most, even when his attention is drawn to the external world of men, or rather women, and nature. He is a vain, mercurial, cynical, unethical individual. Yet for all that, with his verve and vitality, he is a not unattractive person and a poet not without great merit.

Celtis was quite realistic on the whole about his own place and contribution to the art of poetry. He knew that his work did not equal the Latin poets. It was but a preliminary effort to be followed by many greater achievements of those younger poets who would follow him. It is true that his works remained incomplete and had many faults. But one must still concur with the first judgment of literary criticism upon his writings. Asked Vadianus, "should one discard a ring of gold, because its jewel does not sparkle?"[14]

# 10

# Patriot

I T WOULD be a mistake to believe that the German humanists were responsible for the rise in national feeling at
the beginning of the fifteenth century. The truth is that
there had been a gradual rise in popular patriotism during the
preceding two centuries, especially in the borderlands. The
humanists with their ready pens and eloquence added to the
momentum of the patriotic movement.

The Italians were in part responsible for this intensity of
feeling. They had been most indiscreet. Petrarch set an un-
fortunate precedent in his letter to Urban V in which he de-
rided the French as barbarians among whom there could be
no orators or poets. Aeneas Silvius had been exceedingly critical
of the Germans. On the other hand, he unwittingly supplied
a great stimulus to the humanists' national pride by his glowing
description of the cultural progress of Germany under the
aegis of the church. Aeneas' literary protegé, Antonio Cam-
pano, as papal legate for Paul II to the Reichstag of 1471, did
most to stir up animosity. While supposedly in Regensburg
to win the princes' support for a war against the Turks, he
wrote letters to his friends, especially Cardinal Ammanati,
vilifying the Germans, their unfruitful land, rough speech,
rude way of life, and incredible intellectual barbarism. What
a difference between the Danube and the Tiber! The letters

were circulated widely shortly after they were written, though they were not printed until twenty years after his death. They provoked a number of angry responses, among them a reply by Leontorius of the Heidelberg circle. Celtis and his circle were quick to enter into the Italian controversy. Rudolf Agricola had expressed the hope that Germany could free itself of the proud Italians' charges of barbarism and lack of eloquence. Celtis was more aggressive. In his Ingolstadt *Address* he had sounded the call to cultural rivalry with the Italians.

Celtis deplored the condition of the Empire. He regretted that Italy and France were free from the imperium and that the Gauls once subdued by Charlemagne were not only independent, but were infringing upon the territory of the Empire itself. Proud Venice even dared to compare dominions with the Empire.[1] In the north the gateway to the ocean was held by the Danes, and Danzig and Prussia by the Poles. The Elbe had replaced the Vistula as the boundary. In the east powerful peoples lived in slavery—the Bohemians, Moravians, Slovakians, Silesians, and Transylvanian Saxons. With its strange language and heretical religion, Bohemia was like a foreign body in the heart of the Empire. Would that the men of Germany would rise with that ancient spirit which once terrified the Romans and gather together her torn and broken territories.[2] In thus generously defining the frontiers of the Empire, Celtis' conception was based on cultural unity much as the later German romanticists conceived it. He took his cue from Aeneas Silvius, who, in order to demonstrate Germany's great progress, cited its growth beyond the Rhine, Danube, and Vistula.

Like Aeneas, Celtis attacked the princes for their civil strife and the internal dissension which weakened the fatherland and kept it in a constant turmoil. His loyalty was to the *patria*, not to a segment of it. Heinrich Bebel was of the same mind when he described, in an oration to Maximilian, his vision of Germania as an old woman of great size, head bound in laurel wreaths, but attired in torn and soiled robes rousing pity in everyone. In tears she entrusted him with expressing her sorrow to Maximilian and her anger at the disobedience of the princes. The common people could hardly be expected to rise above the level of their rulers. Celtis lamented the luxury and general decline of the age. But if the old virtues were lost they were not beyond recall. For a renewed age of prosperity and culture Celtis looked confidently to the new emperor and the new learning. Celtis believed that with the advent of Maximilian to the throne, the glory of the reborn empire (*renascentis imperii gloria*) would resume its ancient brilliance.

The Germans had already gained renown for their technological achievements and engineering skill. They had contrived new measuring instruments, architectural advances, as evidenced by the history of the cathedral of Milan, gunpowder, and artillery pieces, rivaled only by Leonardo and the Florentine gun-founders. Aeneas Silvius had already attributed the invention of cannons to the Germans. Celtis, like Luther, protested against this new weapon of destruction. All the greater was his pride in the German inventor of printing whom he could not name.

Celtis believed that the time had come when the Muses, like the imperium, would be translated to the North. His humanist colleagues urged him to assume the leadership of this cultural rivalry with the Italians. Accepting with full pride and self-consciousness, he wrote Tucher:

When you read my writings, you will be convinced that I did not send them to you to display my poetic genius. . . , but you will understand that I spared no trouble to accomplish a certain end. For if these efforts do not match those of the Italians, I wish to stimulate and awaken those men among the Germans who excel in learnedness and genius. . . Then the Italians, most effusive in self-praise, will be forced to confess that not only the Roman imperium and arms, but also the splendor of letters has migrated to the Germans.[3]

It was time to dam up the stream of German students descending to Italy for study, especially to Bologna and Padua. The Germans should no longer study canon law in Italy, but rather the Roman law which the Empire alone possessed. During his stay at Linz, while preparing for the presentation of the *Ludus Dianae*, Celtis, together with Longinus and others, debated before Maximilian with the legate of Alexander VI, Francisco Cardulus di Narni, maintaining that a native writer deserved greater credence than a foreigner. If his political thinking was ill-defined, Celtis was at least ready for a cultural declaration of independence.

The attempt to establish the cultural respectability of the German Middle Ages was the chief stimulus to Celtis' search for manuscripts. The German humanists in their concern for medieval history proved themselves to be in a measure independent of the general Renaissance attitude. In this respect they anticipated the reaction of the romantic historicists against the Enlightenment attitude toward the medieval past. Celtis' knowledge of Medieval history was in inverse proportion to his interest in it. It disturbed his scholarly sensitivities not in the least to make Gregory VII a contemporary of Frederick Barbarossa or to leave the Hungarians defeated and broken on the battlefield of Lech before Emperor Charles.

His search for sources was rewarded with two of the most important finds of his generation, a generation which knew so much better than its predecessors what to look for. Both the Roswitha and the Ligurinus were excellent support for his thesis that culture prospered among the Germans also in the dark centuries. In the preface to his Roswitha edition, he explained to Frederick the Wise:

Therefore, when I saw that the many famous and brilliant manuscripts, like so many excellent and prize spoils, were being taken from us and brought by the Italians from Germany to Italy and printed there, I thought to myself that a man born in Hercynia in the heart of Germany and the first German to receive, on your recommendation, most illustrious Prince Frederick, the laurel from the emperor as the ornament and symbol of letters should be dutybound by right of succession and heritage like a skilled hunter to ferret out these codices now lying in obscurity and to present them to my fellow Germans as something to be admired so that they might behold and understand the industry and patient labors which our fathers and progenitors of old devoted to literature and the Christian religion. I was stirred with regret and deep sympathy for the labors of the ancient Germans who wrote these manuscripts with great expense and trouble over seven hundred years ago when we first learned Latin letters (for we at first used Greek letters) together with the Christian religion; for these manuscripts are now through the ignorance and carelessness of our century, in which we follow specious vices, not well enough protected from damaging weather, dust and mold instead of being preserved for literary studies.[4]

The discovery of Roswitha's manuscript was especially gratifying. "It so happened that as I was traveling recently [gathering materials for the *Germania illustrata*] I came by chance to a Benedictine monastery, where I discovered a very old codex written in firm Gothic letters in a woman's hand with the title and inscription of a German virgin and nun of Saxon birth which contained all the works included in the title page and index of this volume. I cannot possibly express the surprise and pleasure at reading the Latin prose and verse of a German woman after six centuries—for that long a time has passed from the time of Otto I to our own day."[5] His reticence to name St. Emmeram as the place of discovery is understandable considering that, in spite of his solemn pledge, he had, seven years later, still not returned the manuscript to the monks who knew what they had given him; in fact, he never gave it back.

The second of Celtis' major finds was a historical document in verse form, the *Ligurinus*. In the last years of his life Celtis drew closer to Konrad Peutinger and the Augsburg circle, visiting them frequently. He traveled to Augsburg in the summer of 1507 to present the manuscript of *Ligurinus* to Peutinger, the city secretary, Marquard von Stein, Provost in Bamberg, Bernhard and Konrad Adelmann von Adelmannsfelden, Matthäus Marschall, and Georg Herwart, members of the *Sodalitas litteraria Augustana*, for printing. He had found the manuscript in the Cistercian monastery of Ebrach not far from his home in Franconia sometime during or before 1501. It too he purloined and never returned; today it is nowhere to be found. Dr. Lorenz Beheim wrote to Pirckheimer when he heard of Celtis' plans for publishing the *Ligurinus:* "He does well in undertaking the publication of *Ligurinus*, for he thereby will turn his thievery to the public good. For I know who was with him when he received that book from the monastery of Ebrach. Although it was only lent to him, he has not returned it to this day."[6]

The *Ligurinus* was made to order for satisfying the patriotic feelings of the humanists. An epic poem of ten books it praised the great deeds of Emperor Frederick Barbarossa in the manner of the *Gesta Friderici* of Otto of Freising and Rahewin. Barbarossa appealed to the humanists as a heroic figure. Cuspinian, for example, considered him the ideal emperor. The formal side of the poem was also not without merit with a certain freedom in the Latin diction and an unusual poetic feeling for analogies taken from nature. The authorship of the poem was in dispute from the very beginning. Celtis left his magic touch also on the *Ligurinus* so that its authenticity has been questioned in modern times. The edition of 1507 was anything but a stellar publishing job, full of mistakes taken directly from the codex with printing errors added. It, too, took on the nature of an omnibus publication including Peutinger's study of the Hohenstauffen genealogy and the like.[7] For all its short-comings, Celtis' *Ligurinus* created a great stir among the humanists and it appeared in five additional editions during the course of the century.

Celtis was interested, like all the humanists, in Roman monuments. He came up with an invaluable find for our knowledge of the Roman world. It was a copy, made possibly by a monk of Colmar in the thirteenth century, of a map of the Roman Empire in the third century. The famous map known as the *Tabula Peutingeriana*, since Celtis willed it to his friend Peutinger who was the greatest inscription collector among the humanists, showed the Roman military roads, the army camps, and cities, giving all distances in Roman miles. Drawn in twelve sections, it depicted the whole Roman world from Spain to the Ganges, though the parts on Spain and Britain are missing, picturing the sea in grey-green and the land in yellow hues. The map can be seen today in the National Library in Vienna. Dr. Eck of Ingolstadt suspected Celtis of having stolen this precious Roman document also.

Celtis naturally pressed his inquiry back beyond the Middle Ages into German antiquity. The chief stimulus for his researches came again from an ancient source discovered in Germany and taken south by the Italians, the *Germania* of Tacitus, published first in Italy in 1470, and in Germany in 1473. Aeneas Silvius was most influential in preparing for the reception of Tacitus. The first description of ancient Germany by a German appeared in 1456 in the *Chronographia Augustensium* of the Augsburg monk Sigismund Meisterlin. In his *Descriptio Sueviae*, he was also the first German to use the *Germania* of Tacitus. The influence of Tacitus became everywhere evident in the historical thinking of the humanists. But the man who really appreciated Tacitus and saw the possibilities for a philosophy of history, which, of course, he never thought through himself, was none other than Conrad Celtis. He lectured on the *Germania* at the University and published an edition of it himself. It is characteristic of him that he relegated the older phantastic fables, as the Trojan descent of the Germans, to silence, and used Tacitus as his basis. But at the same time Tacitus did not satisfy him and he constructed new supplementary theories which were again quite fabulous.

From Tacitus, Celtis learned that the Germans were the original inhabitants of their land—"Germani sunt indigenae."[8] As people indigenous to the land they could make every claim to independence. Influenced by the portrayal of the fraternal *esprit* of the primitive Germans, Celtis adopted an etymology of the name Germani similar to that first suggested by Strabo, who explained that Germani was the same as *fratres*, because the Germani were brothers of the Gauls.

In speaking of the early Germans, Celtis adopted a tone reminiscent of Ovid's reflections on the glory of the state of nature. His conception of the appearance of the early Germans was based upon Tacitus' Nordic ideal. They were tall and strong, light complexioned, with blue eyes and blonde hair. He repeatedly contrasted the decline in ethics with the customs and virtue of the ancient Germans. They wore simple pelt clothing and simple cast-around mantles which covered their hardened bodies. They nourished themselves with simple foods and amused themselves with simple pleasures. No people was more hospitable, more charitable to the needy and the sick. There was no greed and usury, no strife among the princes. They were invincible in battle. Celtis referred to Arminius, following an old legend mistakenly placing the battle with Varrus in the vicinity of Augsburg like most humanists, though he left it to Hutten to make of him a national hero.[9]

Celtis found a counterpart to the primitive Germans in those

unspoiled nature children of the north, the Lapps. That he
drew attention to the neglected north was to his credit, though
he could not refrain from pretending to be its discoverer and
explorer. With a radical Rousseauistic enthusiasm for these
simple nature men, the speechless Lapps, Celtis described his
three-day journey through the dead forests of the land of
perpetual night. Here no one is overheated with wine or corrupted by luxury. No one is swollen with the desire for fame.
No one seeks with murderous intent for gold. No bronze bells
call the people together. No temples resound with song and
flutes and no organ can be heard. Here no jurist twists the law,
no doctor accumulates his blood money, and no tonsured man
plagues the people. They live without money won with strife,
quarrels, and death, with unsheathed weapons and deceptive
art. Would that men were everywhere so fortunate![10] Such
was his vision. But this land of happy illiterates was a strange
Utopia for a humanist. His picture of the early Germans also
presented him with a difficult dilemma. Was an advanced
literate culture a blessing, or was it not?

The solution which he proposed was ingenious, for it at the
same time redeemed the value of literary study and reempha-
sized the independence of the Germans from the culture of
the Latins. If the ancient Germans did not originally speak
Greek, they were at least led to culture by the druids who
spoke Greek and lived the Greek way of life. The druids
brought the people still in the state of nature to farming and
the breeding of cattle, private property, and to monotheism.
Their successors were the monks who built their monasteries
where the old oracles had stood in the deep woods, a cultural
development which took place under the Charleses, Arnulfs,
and the Ottos. These German emperors were the successors of
Tuisco, the founder of the German nation.[11] Celtis' Greek
druid theory found ready acceptance by a number of hu-

manists and contributed to the general confusion about German antiquity.

Celtis habitually used antique names for people, tribes, and localities, conflating the past with the present. Many of these he borrowed from the *Germania*, often applying them quite incorrectly. The skeptical Agrippa of Nettesheim in his essay on the vanity of historical knowledge singled Celtis out for special mention as the contrivor of many highly dubious etymologies. The work which Celtis intended to be his masterpiece, the *Germania illustrata*, in fact, was designed to be a descriptive eulogy of ancient and modern Germany, combining historical narrative with geographical and topographical essays. The model for this work was obviously Flavio Biondo's *Italia illustrata*. He would have organized it on the pattern already familiar from the *Amores* and would have embellished it with lyric selections, though it was possibly to be done in prose. With the *Amores* Celtis published a sample which should satisfy the Emperor until the whole ambitious work could appear, the *Germania generalis*. It described in a poetic flight the creation of the world by the Demogorgon; Germany's position in the temperate zone where only labor will yield rewards; the native peoples, warlike, pious, trustworthy, and true; the stars; the four main rivers; the three chief mountain ranges; and, finally, the cultivation of the land which was transcending its early primitive state of culture. This was only a fragment. Celtis never completed the project.

The idea did not die with Celtis, but was taken up in Nuremberg by Pirckheimer and his circle. The plan of the *Germania illustrata* culminated in the geographical work of Sebastian Münster, the *Germaniae descriptio* of 1530, and the more historical work of Johannes Aventine, the *Zeitbuch über gans Teutschland*. None of these succeeding attempts, however, came close to realizing Celtis' ambitious program. The requirements of such cultural history combined with geographical learning such as Celtis envisioned was beyond the historical scholarship of the time. With the passing of the years and the stress of crisis, humanism lost the verve necessary to attack a project of such giant proportions.

Geographical lore and ethnography always intrigued the well-traveled Celtis. He was alert to the peculiar characteristics of the landscapes and interested in identifying especially peoples and places cited by the classic authors. He even mentions in passing the peculiarities of the curly-haired Negro, the Indian, and the products of Arabia, Japan, and China. He was quick to explain ethnic characteristics in terms of climatic influences. He wrote of the division of the earth into zones and "climates," a theory held by some into the seventeenth century. He praised Ptolemy who had described sixteen climates or belts within parallel circles, each separated from the next by a difference of half an hour in the length of the longest day. Celtis held the earth to be round and immobile, with the planets moving about it in perfect spheres. But his preoccupation with Germany and Ptolemy blinded him to the biggest news of the century—the discovery of the New World.

Johann Kollauer, royal secretary and a member of the Augsburg Sodality, wrote Celtis on May 4, 1503 from Antwerp about the most amazing reports he had ever heard.

We have arrived in this land where no day passes on which I would not call you a thousand times. You would here see, among many other noteworthy things, Portuguese sailors who relate astounding tales. You would wonder at the absurd statements of all the ancient writers who have asserted that things are not to be found in human nature, unless they themselves had discovered and seen them. You would see here another kind of map for navigating to the antarctic pole and men who would relate to you marvelous and unheard of things. Our lord overseer Matthäus Lang has drawn that table which you will soon see, when you join us. I am unable to write about all that we have seen and heard. Another world has been found unknown to the ancients! All the more I exhort you, because the shortage of time does not allow a longer letter, that you come to us all the more speedily. Here you will enjoy the delight of talking with the men who have seen it. That you do this as speedily as possible is my greatest wish. . . Farewell and love me.[12]

Celtis, leave your classic authors and their books behind. Go and see! Celtis did not visit Antwerp. Nor did he inquire further into the matter or ever refer to the New World in a single line. His faith in the ancients was unshaken; the pillars of Hercules remained for him the *ultima tellus*.

Celtis planned an epic poem to Theoderic the Ostrogoth which, like the *Aneid*, was to be a saga of the heroic period of the Germans. Aside from the good intention, nothing further is known of it. His service to Maximilian's genealogical histories were hardly more productive. He did travel to Sponheim in 1502 with the old-time court historiographer, Ladislaus Suntheim, seeking materials for the Habsburg genealogy. But Suntheim did not find him a satisfactory colleague for a labor so pedestrian and dispensed with his assistance.

Celtis was no historian in the professional sense of the word. He lacked the quiet and stability, the self-discipline, necessary. But, through his personal influence as a teacher full of enthusiasm for the German past, he made an important contribution to history. He and his Vienna humanists added to the mounting tide of German patriotism which was to play such a crucial role in the coming Protestant revolt. Also, Ulrich von Hutten visited Vienna shortly before his Italian journey only three years after Celtis' death. Thus, he too may have come in contact with Celtis' patriotic notions.

It is true that Celtis had only vague political ideas and was more a proponent of cultural autonomy. But, if Celtis the patriot was far from the nationalism of the present century, he was equally as far from the universalism of the Middle Ages. He could never have written as Erasmus to his Brabant countryman: "Where you fare well, there is your fatherland."

# Philosopher

IF MENTAL DISCIPLINE and capacity for sustained thought are essential attributes of a formal philosopher, then Celtis was far from being one. On the big questions his thinking was protean and inconclusive. He showed a grand indifference to the need for consistency. In a remarkable way he combined Platonic mysticism with an Aristotelian view of nature. He savagely attacked the church, its clergy, and dogma, yet performed his religious duties as though no trace of doubt marred the serenity of a simple faith. He lead an openly immoral life, if not so successfully as he boasted, and at the end turned to the comforts of a pious death. In a very real way these contradictions were not his alone, but less obviously those of his whole generation.

By philosophy in the broadest sense of the word, Celtis meant all humanist knowledge. Philosophy was that learning which opened a way into the secrets of nature and of the higher life to which rhetoric and the divine poetry held the key. Those gifted with sufficient virtue and genius (*virtus ingeniumque*) could achieve true philosophic insight and the full life. In that broad sense of the word he looked to philosophy as the humanist program of reform, a reflection of his own Faustian drive toward all knowledge. "How beautiful it is to read great books and to enrich life with good studies!"

The philosophy in the narrower sense which pervaded his literary effusions was antique-naturalistic influenced strongly by nebulous emanations from Ficino's neoplatonism. He loved to be addressed as a "doctor of the threefold philosophy." But of the three—spiritual, moral, and natural philosophy—it was the third which intrigued him most. The study of nature could be truly rewarding only to those enlightened by a knowledge of the divine philosopher Plato. The threefold philosophy meant for him also the learning to be found in the Latin, Greek, and Hebrew writings. With the exception of Wimpheling, who still spoke an earnest word in behalf of Aristotle, Melanchthon, and a few others, the German humanists from Agricola on considered themselves promoters of Plato, or more properly, of neoplatonism, according to their lights. Celtis was in the forefront, at least in sound and fury. In reality his limited knowledge of Greek kept him from consulting Plato directly, and the intervention of neoplatonism made his acquaintance with the divine philosopher even more remote. His Platonism was a poor thing.

Like Virgil, Celtis felt impelled to learn the causes of things. This ideal of the intellectual pursuit under Lucretian influence inspired the imperial poets, Celtis' cultural heroes. The question of the inner essence of the universe, its principle of unity, captured his imagination as it had the early Greek nature philosophers. And, like them, he propounded theories far removed from experimental foundation. How did the *vaga semina mundi* develop from the lap of chaos? What were the hidden powers of nature? He believed he was philosophizing in all seriousness when he treated poetically astronomical or physical questions.

Celtis was obsessed with the neoplatonic conception of the universe as an organism bound by sympathetic ties. It was the highly spiritualized Renaissance view of the world exemplified by Ficino which influenced men of no mean scientific stature as Copernicus, Bruno, and Kepler. In poetic prose Ficino described this macro-microcosm, the sympathy of the world above and that below, how the world breathed in the heavenly rays on plants, stones, and even the bodies and souls of men. He wrote:

Man is the earthly star in a cloudy covering and the stars are heavenly people. . . To the song of the joyous heavenly spirits, as the Pythagoreans believe, the spheres lead the dances. . . When the stars laugh, everything in heaven and earth laughs. . . Light is the laughter of heaven and expresses the joy of the heavenly spirits. . . And from the laughing stars as from the eyes of divine minds friendly and happy rays travel influencing the seeds of all living things.

Celtis was entirely taken by this view of nature. "Everything in the world has its own special ray, since all the stars of the heaven move under the earth. But the human spirit excels every living thing through its rays, for its own seeds rise from related stars and it is said to stand near to the aetherial gods." He thought such phenomena as the tides might be due to the regular breathing of the world as a living organism. Many problems of nature could never be answered with certainty. "Who can give sure account of the causes of all natural appearances? Weak is our conjecture, shaky and uncertain our combination."[1] Celtis was only a poet. Perhaps this uncertainty prompted him to seek assurance in the stars.

This atmosphere of neoplatonic nature-mysticism was most conducive to astrological belief. The fifth-century grammarian Macrobius helped convince Celtis that man's fate was controlled by the seven stars. The stars, through the mixture of their rays, determine the characteristics of things, binding and loosening body and soul. The spirit bound to its "spheres" from which the life-power and heartbeats proceed is like the mechanism of a clock revolving and striking each hour on time.[2] One of the purposes of his *Amores*, Celtis observed in the preface, was to show the influence of the stars on human life. His whole life was lived under the spell of this sidereal delusion. Unlike Ficino, who in his *De vita triplici* warned against the bitterness of melancholy, or Dürer, who included the idea in his woodcut of *Philosophia* in the *Amores*, Celtis was not given to brooding over the melancholy influence of Saturn. He was far too sanguine, or, rather, choleric for that. All this makes his occasional attacks against the astrologers quite unimpressive. The combination of mild protest against grotesque aspects of astrology and a basic belief in it was common among the humanists. Pico was quite exceptional. Humanist astrology renewed from sources in late antiquity was clearly a regrettable case of cultural atavism. How could a man of Celtis' philosophic stature rise above it? Instead it gave him a new opportunity to indulge his poetic penchant for phantasy.

Similarly Pythagorean number-mysticism held for him the same fascination as for Pico, Reuchlin, or Trithemius, though he became less involved in it than they. Somewhat more elevating was his attitude toward witchcraft and magic. He does, to be sure, play with the idea of magic in his poetry, but he has nothing but scorn for its practitioners. Unlike Trithemius, Bebel, and other humanists, Celtis was not guilty of adding fuel to the pyre on which many poor wretches were to burn.

The natural philosopher probing deep and secret causes had inevitably to confront the problem of free will and determination. Fate or Fortuna played a role in Germany during the fifteenth and sixteenth centuries similar to that in Italy. That role was problematical and few thinkers in the South or North thought it through with the vigor of Machiavelli. The problem demanded much attention in the high Middle Ages with the introduction of terms as Moira, Fatum, Tyche-Fortuna. It proved no less difficult conceptually for the poor philosophers of the Renaissance. Already in Dante, Fortuna appeared in a double aspect—as purely a goddess of luck favoring all alike, and as an incomprehensible fate defying all human calculation. Petrarch touched on the problem only occasionally and then spoke in contradictory terms. The German humanists wrestled with the problem in terms of inexorable fate, human virtue, and divine providence. Most of them never got much beyond identifying fate with the changeableness and transiency of all things, the incalculableness of the powers presiding over life.

Nor did Celtis arrive at a satisfying solution of the three factors at play. In an ode on fate and felicity he describes the working of impenetrable fortune. Only he who sits alone on Olympus, mixing joys with sorrows, knows and governs the causes in our lives, gives and denies. Although our hearts are unable to see through the dark shadows, he has actually established proud fate to give his certain gifts in all things. These come at the appointed time, even though the windows have been firmly closed. The politician in the king's court is suddenly ruined, the poet rises unexpectedly to great fame, the prosperous merchant perishes with his ship bound for the Indies. One married man is left childless; another has too many sons. One man, choosing private life, is destined to rule; another, preferring the ancestral home, dies an exile on a foreign shore. One dies by the sword, another is burned alive, a third hangs on a cross, a fourth is twisted on a wheel. Thus, drunken fortune plays, oppressing the mind with care, joyous hope, or fear. The wise man must daringly persist with a vigor of mind equal to it. This was Celtis' most usual counsel. To young Fusilius he wrote: "Learn to spurn the favor of unstable fortune and to bear hardships and you will live out your days in happiness."[3] The activist in him usually won out. The virtue which

he verbally opposed to fortune was often more the pious life
which promises bliss than the *virtú* of the author of the *Prince*.
Fate was, after all, in God's hands, a thought which should give
man peace of mind. In an epigram to Jove, the all highest,
Celtis beseeches the ruler of destiny to reveal the laws by
which he governs, lest oppressed men believe that all things
are directed by capricious steps and stand under no rule. Other-
wise destiny will remain forever blind in a way opposed to
virtue and limited by no law. All this was far too much for
Celtis. "Whatever the truth is, may we seize the joys of a
doubtful life, since it will return to nothing, for it once was
nothing."[4]

In view of his uncertainties and the poverty of his positive
philosophy, the self-assurance with which Celtis attacked the
scholastic philosophers might seem surprising. The answer is
that Celtis did not oppose scholasticism on a philosophic basis.
He opposed it rather because of its different cultural ideal. It
was the interests and method of the scholastics to which Celtis
objected, not the validity of their premises and conclusions. It
was for this reason that he could teach on university faculties
that were predominantly scholastic with only occasional frictions and unpleasantries. In fact, Celtis was sufficiently tolerant
about the issues at stake to plan a work which would effect
harmony between the poets and theologians, the *Parnassus
biceps*, a book which was either never begun or subsequently
lost.[5]

Celtis reveled in the offensive and took the greatest delight
in criticizing the clergy. His attacks, as typical of popular
satirical literature of the time as of specifically humanist writings, were direct and usually humorless. Like the fiery Hutten,
thirty years his junior, Celtis gave expression to an anti-clericalism prompted by a patriotic motivation. It was moral indignation against laxity and abuse, though it came with ill-

grace from an open lecher like Celtis, as well as opposition to the exploitation of his Germans by clerics and the curia which stirred his anger. He himself, like Hutten who published a new edition of it, had a copy of Lorenzo Valla's *De donatione constantiniana* and so had reason to doubt the foundation of papal power.

Celtis struck even nearer to the heart of the sacramental-sacerdotal system with his jibes at transubstantiation. Fasts and prayers were for the hooded monks, not for the humanist comrades. The priests anxiously try to suppress the possession of religious books by the people, but in the future not only clerics, but all the people shall have a knowledge of divine wisdom. Everyone can now read the Holy Scriptures spread by printing: "Now there are so many printed books in Germany that every inn has a copy of the Holy Scriptures."[6] Such expressions show clearly that Celtis opposed abuse as a patriot and regretted the externalization of doctrine. But they show also that he did not feel bound by the inner dogma of the church.

A universalist element in his spiritual philosophy is evident in his praise of the old philosophers and poets who achieved such harmony in the light of nature and of grace. He consistently used classic names for God and the saints and classic myths and phrases for Christian references. God the Father was Jupiter, and Mary, the mother of the Thunderer. Mercury was the guide to the world beyond. Heaven was the Elysian fields, hell, the nether world of the Furies guarded by Cerberus and ruled by the judge Radamanthus. A mind preoccupied with antique literature and philosophy would inevitably be conditioned also by antique religious thought. This was true of Celtis to a greater extent perhaps than he himself knew. This is evident particularly in his idea of God, of immortality, and of justification by civil virtue.

Is there a God? If so, what is his nature? These are radical questions for one standing within the received tradition. The closing of the "Carmen Saeculare," a poem hailing the advent of the new century, is indicative of his mood. "Thou in whom the wandering stars of the heavens rest and all which is upon the earth, lend a favorable ear to our petitions. Thy name and thy power we are not able to recognize. Whoever Thou art, be kind to Germany in whose cities many altars pour up smoke to Thee." God's name and essence were unknowable. He was an abscondite God, who was not to be found in churches. And yet he was a God present everywhere in nature and within man. Celtis' most radical ode expresses his views clearly:

### To Sepulus the Superstitious

*You marvel that I never move my lips in any church*
*Murmuring through my teeth in prayer.*
*The reason is that the great divine Will of Heaven*
*Hears the small inner voice.*
*You marvel that you so seldom see me*
*Dragging my feet into the temples of the gods.*
*God is within us. I do not need to meditate on Him*
*In painted churches.*
*You marvel that I love to seek the open waters*
*And the warm sun.*
*It is there that the mighty image of omnipotent Jupiter*
*      appears to me.*
*There are the highest temples of God.*
*The woods are pleasing to the Muses, a city is hateful*
*      to poets*
*And so is the evil of milling crowds.*
*Go now and deride my gods with your foolish words,*
*My blustering Sepulus!*

Here, surely, is a clear expression of that humanist universal theism which, if popularized, might have posed a serious threat to the sacramental-sacerdotal system of the medieval church. In another flippant ode addressed to Crispus, the buffoon of the poets, Celtis contrasted the beauties of worship in nature with the noisy shouting of a dullard priest preaching to a crowd of stupid people.[7]

It was especially in nature that Celtis sought for God. "Does God concern himself with the world, at work within its mass, or has He withdrawn from his work, so that all depends on chance and fate and God comes staggering after with an uncertain step?" he asked. His search for the divine was generally associated with an inquiry into natural causation. "I would," cried Celtis, "behold the flaming fire of heaven, of the sea, and of the earth and I would learn to know the causes of the wind, the fog, and the snow! I would find Thee, Father of all things, through whom the immeasurable world has been established and whose nod would send it reeling off into chaos again! Omnipresent the Spirit sweeps through the world, enlivening every single part, whom only pure minds are able to see and apprehend."[8] In the dedication of the *Amores*, Celtis celebrates love, the neoplatonic Eros, as the cosmic principle, the love of the Creator for the creature, the love which the philosophers depict as active in fire, water, steam, and air in originating the world. "We, however, name Him the highest God who made man from a lump of earth and slime and implanted in him as in all living beings, plants and seeds, yes in inanimate things as stones and colors, the power and characteristics of love, so that they as a result of a natural relationship and a silent inner agreement seek and desire to join each other." This was not far from Lucretius' ode to Venus as the creatrix of all things. This orientation explains in part Celtis' enthusiasm for the religion of the early Germans.

The conception of God in nature and within men reflected in these passages is typical of the views of Florentine neoplatonism. But for his idea of Eros as the divine principle of unity, Celtis expressly acknowledges Ovid's *Metamorphosis* as the source of his inspiration. Ovid, too, wrote of the "god within us."[9] There was less of the true seeker in Celtis, less of the mystical desire and thirst of the soul for the communion with the divine than in Ficino. He was less a religious man than Ficino. He was rather the bold and unreflecting poet who dares to seek God where he would. He was so little the god-seeker even in the aestheticized Florentine ascetic sense.

Celtis' radical estrangement from orthodox otherworldiness led him to question the destiny and even the existence of the soul after death. He thought that the punishments of hell, the hot regions of Pluto, or a severe cold for sentient shades were the inventions of the slothful priests with which they rule the blind hearts of the masses. One should despise their murmurings. Yet he was not without the fear of a divine judgment. "Despiser of the gods, beware lest Fortune with wandering feet assault you. For no mortal can long safely prevail as a despiser of the gods."[10] One type of immortality alone was assured—the immortal fame of the poet. Desire for fame, called by Dante "lo gran disio dell' eccellenza" and by Boccaccio "perpetuandi nominis desiderium," was for Celtis a great driving power. Fame would rescue him from the abyss of nothingness and assure for him a life beyond death.

Only the life of virtue gives man security, the promise of a celestial seat, and removes fear of Styx. Celtis' admonitions have all the makings of a morality religion, but Celtis could not bear the strain of moralizing. In an ode to Sebaldus praising the active life, proposing educational reform, urging the care of the temple and of its images, and lauding the gift of a good conscience, he concludes, "but refrain, Clio, from describing the fate of wicked men with a more severe song, restore Bacchus, who is accustomed to play to more gentle muses!" Again and again he admonishes the comrades to banish cares with sleep, sadness with wine, and to seize the joys of a short life which flees like a shadow.[11] What he has to say about the independence of man from external influences, of virtue and self-control, is typically humanist. Coming from him it is less than convincing.

The radical departures in his natural and spiritual philosophy and the effeteness of his moral philosophy did not prevent Celtis from paying his formal respects to traditional Christianity and the church. He spoke with concern of the fortunes of "our religion." Indeed, he placed credulity in medieval religious practices soon to be swept away by the Reformation. Like Agricola and almost all the other German humanists, Celtis composed poems to the saints. He gave his greatest attention to the Virgin Mary, whose icon he placed at his door. With the upper Rhenish humanists he entered the lists against the Dominicans in favor of the doctrine of the immaculate conception of Mary. He vacillated between criticism and credulity about miracles. Weak and feverish with disease, he sought and found at least temporary relief by pilgrimages to the shrine of the Virgin on the Danube. He traveled to the shrine of Alt-Oetting in Bavaria which is still visited by thousands of pilgrims each year.

Celtis died of the French disease on February 4, 1508, piously and in a most Christian manner, his friend, Thomas Resch, assures us. He was carried in a grand procession, with the entire company of Vienna University professors and students in attendance, to St. Stephen's cathedral. The son of a peasant, he lies buried not far from the tomb of Emperor Frederick III, who had crowned him the first poet laureate of Germany. Thus died a man of eloquence and a philosopher in the arms of the church.

Celtis knew that he had not achieved the greatest heights of artistic creation. He wrote:

> My songs which I have sung in German lands,
> Equal and excel, oh young men of the future! [12]

Little did he dream that the songs his Germans would sing were not the precious pieces of the Latin poets, but the fervent hymns of the Reformation.

Was Celtis a free, enlightened thinker, a champion of reason and individual liberty breaking the bondage of ecclesiastical authority and medieval superstition? To answer the question as did the nineteenth-century liberal historians reveals an essentially unhistorical way of thinking. A direct affirmation is oversimplification. What constitutes intellectual revolt varies, of course, with historical epochs. There is a difference not only of degree, but of kind. In many ways with his Platonic idealism, Celtis was more of a believer than his rationalistic scholastic contemporary, though less in an established pattern. The humanists had a pattern and a conformity of their own. He was clearly not the militant man of reason questioning the supernatural. It was less that he despised the saints than that he raised the heroes of classic literature to their level. Nor, it may be noted in this connection, is it either historical or just to blame Celtis and his fellows with arriving merely at a "series of half-solutions." The ambivalence in many of his attitudes toward the big questions was not hypocrisy. It was an honest reflection of his confusion about matters for which he had no final criterion for judgment and scarcely the vocabulary for articulation. Celtis merely posed a "perhaps." For his time, indeed, he was a free spirit. That freedom was far from the skepticism, liberalism, and rationalism which D. F. Strauss and the Burckhardtians enthusiastically acclaimed, when they christened Celtis the German arch-humanist.

NOTES

# Notes

*Mortuus ille quidem sed longum vivus in aevum*
*Colloquitur doctis per sua scripta viris*
 —Epitaphium Celtis ab ipso compositum

THE FIRST biography of Celtis was included in the 1513 edition of his *Odes, Conradi Celtis per sodalitatem litterariam Rhenanam vita*. Actually only a fragment, the first part was biographical and the second was a collection of maxims with a list of his most important works, the date of his death, and a notice of the provisions of his testament. The authors of the seventeenth and eighteenth centuries for the most part followed the *Vita* uncritically. H. A. Erhard, *Geschichte des Wiederaufblühens wissenschaftlicher Bildung*, II (Magdeburg, 1830), 1, note 1, lists the older literature. At about the same time, Ladislaus Endlicher devoted two studies to Celtis, *Hormayrs Archiv für Geschichte*, XII (1821), 381ff., and *Jahrbücher der Literatur*, XLV (1829), 141ff., which corrected some errors, but introduced new ones of equal gravity.

Far superior to these was Engelbert Klüpfel's *De vita et scriptis Conradi Celtis Protucii*, 2 volumes (Freiburg i.B., 1827). Klüpfel, born in the same town as Celtis, was attracted to him by a kind of antiquarian interest. An Augustinian monk and professor at Freiburg University, he lovingly devoted a great part of his life to collecting source materials on Celtis, but he died in 1811 without having published his work. Between 1813 and 1827 it was published in twelve programs of Freiburg University, and then in 1827 in two volumes with J. C. Ruef and C. Zell as editors. It remained, however, a rich store of source materials rather than an organic biography. Unfortunately, the fact that Klüpfel indulged his fancy

in composing probable answers of Celtis to the letters he had received led to many distortions, for they were accepted as genuine
by uncritical scholars until recent times.

Later in the century a Vienna professor, Joseph Ritter von
Aschbach, devoted himself to the study of Celtis with highly questionable results. He stirred up much interest and an acrimonious
controversy with his pronouncement in a lecture published in
1867, *Roswitha und Conrad Celtes*, that Celtis and his friends had
actually forged the Roswitha drama manuscript from a patriotic
motive. In a second study, *Die früheren Wanderjahre des Conrad
Celtes* (Vienna, 1869), he attempted to bring order into the highly
confused account of Klüpfel. But here he proved to be as credulous
as in the former case he had been skeptical, accepting literally the
poetic fictions of Celtis' *Amores* as a major source. In a third study,
*Geschichte der Wiener Universität*, II, *Die Wiener Universität
und ihre Humanisten im Zeitalter Kaiser Maximilians I* (Vienna,
1877), he undertook with only indifferent success to depict the
impact of humanist thought on the university.

There followed then a spate of monographic studies on various
phases of Celtis' life and activities. Of these, an excellent character
study of Celtis as a hero of neo-classical culture deserves special
mention—Friedrich von Bezold's article "Konrad Celtis, der
deutsche Erzhumanist," *Historische Zeitschrift*, XLIX (1883),
republished in his book *Aus Mittelalter und Renaissance* (Munich,
1918). Friedrich Moth in a Danish dissertation, *Conradus Celtis
Protucius: Tysklands første laurbaerkronede Digter* (Copenhagen,
1898), succeeded in resolving a number of vexing questions. It was
a distinct handicap that he could not yet make use of Gustav
Bauch's fundamental studies of the German universities. Of his
many researches, those most relevant for Celtis were his *Deutsche
Scholaren in Krakau* (Breslau, 1901), *Die Anfänge des Humanismus in Ingolstadt* (Munich, 1901), and *Die Reception des Humanismus in Wien* (Breslau, 1903). In spite of certain false notions,
his work will remain a basic contribution to our knowledge of the
period. In 1901 Bauch was entrusted with the editing of Celtis'
correspondence. He became preoccupied with preparatory studies,
however, and did not complete the project before his death in
1924.

Two recent studies of Celtis merit special mention. Harald

Drewinc includes an able sketch of Celtis in his little book, *Vier Gestalten aus dem Zeitalter des Humanismus* (St. Gallen, 1946). Of even greater interest is the first book in English on Celtis by Leonard Forster, *Selections from Conrad Celtis, 1459-1508* (Cambridge, 1948), presenting a happy choice of poems and the Ingolstadt Address with a translation and commentary.

The publication of new critical editions of Celtis' works and letters is an event of the greatest importance: Karl Hartfelder, *Fünf Bücher Epigramme von Konrad Celtes* (Berlin, 1881); Albert Werminghoff, *Conrad Celtis und sein Buch über Nürnberg* (Freiburg i.B., 1921), with a critical edition of the *Norimberga;* Hans Rupprich, *Conradus Celtis Protucius: Oratio in Gymnasio in Ingelstadio publice recitata, cum carminibus ad Orationem pertinentibus* (Leipzig, 1932), in the series *Bibliotheca Scriptorum Medii Recentisque Aevorum, Saecula XV-XVI,* Ladislaus Juhasz, ed.; F. Pindter, *Conradus Celtis Protucius, Quattuor Libri Amorum secundum quattuor latera Germaniae,* etc. (Leipzig, 1934), also in the *Bibliotheka Scriptorum* series; F. Pindter, *Conradus Celtis Protucius, Libri Odarum Quattuor,* etc. (Leipzig, 1937), in the *Bibliotheka Scriptorum* series; Virginia Gingerick, "The *Ludus Dianae* of Conrad Celtes," *Germanic Review,* XV (1940); Felicitas Pindter, *Conradus Celtis Protucius, Ludi Scaenici* (Budapest, 1945), *Bibliotheka Scriptorum* series. Pending in the same series is a new edition of the *Libri epigrammatum quinque,* F. Pindter, ed. Above all, the appearance of *Der Briefwechsel des Konrad Celtis* (Munich, 1934), edited by the distinguished Vienna scholar, Hans Rupprich, has at last made available in an excellent scholarly edition his complete extant correspondence.

## Chapter 1—The First Poet Laureate

1. Ode III, 21.
2. Gerhard Ritter, *Geschichte der Heidelberger Universität* (Heidelberg, 1936), I, 464ff., is the chief advocate of revisionism.
3. Celtis had apparently previously written a *Tractatus de preceptis rhetoris,* but it is not extant. K. Hartfelder, "Der Humanist Celtis als Lehrer," *Neue Jahrbücher für Philologie und Pädagogik* (1883), CXXVIII, 303, describes the *Ars* primarily as a teaching aid. It appeared in two editions: the first in Leipzig, 24 folios, Summer 1486; the second also in Leipzig, 20 folios, after April 1487.
4. *Lucy anei senece cordubensis hercules furens tragedia prima in-*

*cipit* and *Lucy Anei Senece Cordubensis tragedia secunda Cena Thiestis Incipit.*

5. K. Schottenloher, "Kaiserliche Dichterkrönungen im Heiligen Römischen Reiche Deutscher Nation," *Papsttum und Kaisertum*, A. Brackmann, ed. (Munich, 1926), pp. 648ff.

6. Epod 1.

7. The diploma is to be found in a copy in the *codex epistolarum*, Österreichische Nationalbibliothek codex 3448, and in Br. 7, pp. 14ff. (Br. = *Briefwechsel*, Rupprich ed.). J. Aschbach, *Die früheren Wanderjahre*, doubts that this diploma is genuine. His arguments are inconclusive, however.

8. Ode I, 5, lines 81-84.

9. Br. 10, pp. 18f.

10. Josef Truhlář, *Listář Bohuslava Hasísteinského Z Lobkovic* (Prague, 1893), ep. 10, p. 11, and ep. 11, p. 12. The date 1486 given by Truhlar is probably inaccurate.

11. Oratio Lipsiae habita, "Conradum Celten paene hostiliter expulistis." G. Bauch, *Geschichte des Leipziger Frühhumanismus* (Leipzig, 1899), p. 20, gives the date as 1511. See G. Bauch, "Die Vertreibung des Johannes Rhagius Aesticampianus aus Leipzig," *Archiv für Litteraturgeschichte*, XIII (1885) p. 21.

12. G. Bauch, *Die Universität Erfurt im Zeitalter des Frühhumanismus* (Breslau, 1904), pp. 122ff., contains Questenberg's poem.

13. Br. 315, pp. 568f.

14. *Ars versificandi*, 1486 ed., p. 47. This edition of the poem is contained in the Nationalbibliothek Codex 9696, folio 20$^v$, of uncertain hand and date.

## CHAPTER 2—The Wandering Humanist

1. Ep. II, 46 (Ep. = Epigram).

2. Ep. IV, 25; Ep. III, 13; Ep. III, 12; Ep. V, 92; Am. III, 8, lines 37-44 (Am. = Amores); Ep. II, 47.

3. Ep. II, 48.

4. "An Open Letter to the Christian Nobility," *Three Treatises* (Philadelphia, 1947), p. 57.

5. Ep. III, 40.

6. G. Bauch, *Deutsche Scholaren in Krakau*, p. 38. Ep. I, 90: Ad gymnasium Cracouiense, dum orare vellet. C. Morawski, *Histoire de L'université de Cracovie* 3 vols. (Paris, 1900-5), III, 64, n. 2, describes another such a poem by Celtis in a manuscript in Leningrad discovered by M. Fijalek announcing a lecture on epistelography to be given Thursday, July 23, at the eleventh hour "in aula Hungarorum." The document is dated 1489.

7. G. Bauch, "Laurentius Corvinus, der Breslauer Stadtschreiber und Humanist," *Zeitschrift für Geschichte und Alterthum Schlesiens,* XVII, 231ff. G. Bauch, "Schlesien und die Universität Krakau im XV. und XVI. Jahrhundert," *Zeitschrift des Vereins für Geschichte Schlesiens,* XLI, 316, no. 116. Compare Br. 217, pp. 361f., n. 1. Other students were Sigismund Gossinger, Urbanus Prebusinus, Vinzenz Lang, Johannes Sommerfeld.

8. Ep. I, 48; Ep. I, 13; Ode I, 23, lines 6-8; Ep. I, 45; Am. I, 3, line 14; Ep. I, 12; Ep. I, 44; Ep. I, 56; Ep. I, 14; Ep. I, 47; Ep. I, 43; Ep. I, 29; Ep. I, 44.

9. On heavy drinking in Breslau, Ep. I, 55; on the arms and avarice of the Bishop of Breslau, Ep. IV, 62. On Prague, Br. 11, pp. 20ff., n. 1; Ep. I, 72; Ep. I, 71; Ep. I, 65; Ep. I, 67.

10. Ep. I, 68; Ep. I, 70; Ep. I, 64; Ep. I, 69; Am. II, 4, lines 26-30; Ep. I, 73; Ep. I, 75; Ep. I, 76; Ep. I, 78; Br. 11, p. 22; Ode I, 27.

11. Ep. I, 85; Ep. I, 86; Ep. I, 81; Ep. I, 65; Ep. I, 67; Br. 11, p. 21, lines 18f.; Br. 11, pp. 20ff.; Br. 13, pp. 25f.; Br. 14, pp. 27f.; Ep. I, 82; Ep. I, 63.

12. Am. I, 3, lines 61f.

## CHAPTER 3—Ingolstadt and the Reform of University Education

1. The correspondence of Celtis and Tucher is contained in the Münchener Universitäts-Bibliothek, Cod. MS 782. It was published for the first time in K. Hartfelder, "Konrad Celtes und Sixtus Tucher," *Zeitschrift für vergleichende Litteraturgeschichte und Renaissance-litteratur,* N.F. III (1890), 332ff.

2. G. Bauch, *Die Anfänge des Humanismus in Ingolstadt,* pp. 27ff.

3. It is still extant in his own handwriting, Münchener Universitäts-Bibliothek, Cod. MS 782; Br. 32, pp. 55ff.; Ep. V, 18: Academiae, is a poetic invitation to a lecture on Cicero. See also Ep. III, 103.

4. Ep. V, 20, suggests a preoccupation with Horace, although the reference to his illness makes a later date seem probable. In Br. 33, pp. 57f., Celtis asks to borrow Ptolemy from Tucher. Compare Ep. III, 111; Ep. V, 11. Teaching epigrams, Ep. IV, 28; Ep. I, 16; Ep. IV, 31; Ep. V, 21.

5. Br. 40, pp. 66ff., lines 31-35, from Theodoricus Rhenanus, Zwettl, Sept. 21, 1492.

6. Maria Humula, "Beiträge zum humanistischen Bildungsprogramm des Peter Luder, Rudolf Agricola und Konrad Celtis," Vienna dissertation, 1946, attempts a comparison of the three educational programs, though with serious errors.

7. The version printed with the *Oratio* is reprinted in Iohannes Rupprich, ed., *Conradus Celtis Protucius Oratio*. The version printed as Ode I, 11, in the 1513 edition is reprinted in F. Pindter, ed., *Conradus Celtis Protucius Libri Odarum Quattuor*.

8. Br. 39, pp. 65f.

9. Br. 58, pp. 95ff.; Br. 59, pp. 97f. In a pedagogical poem of eighteen distichs composed almost certainly for his schoolboys, Celtis laid down disciplinary rules he expected to be followed, the *leges ingenuorum et studiosorum adolescentium*, Ep. I, 8. How far he was from the spirit of Hegius and Deventer!

## CHAPTER 4—Nuremberg and the *Norimberga*

1. M. Herrmann, *Die Rezeption des Humanismus in Nürnberg* (Berlin, 1898), pp. 1ff., is concerned with revising the too sanguine picture of Nuremberg as a center of humanism.

2. P. Joachimsen, *Geschichtsauffassung und Geschichtschreibung in Deutschland unter dem Einfluss des Humanismus* (Leipzig, 1910), p. 155. On Schedel, compare Br., p. 99, note 2; H. Bösch, "Eine projektiert gewesene zweite Ausgabe der sogennante Schedelschen Chronik," *Mitteilungen aus dem Germanischen National-museum*, I (Nuremberg, 1886), 382, cited in A. Werminghoff, *Conrad Celtis*, p. 26, note 2.

3. The Norimberga excelled its successors as well, for example, Johannes Cochlaeus, *De Norimberga*, chapter IV in his *Germania* (1512) using Celtis, Christoph Scheurl's letter of 1516 on the city constitution, Hans Sachs's *Lobspruch der Stadt Nürnberg*, 1530, Eobanus Hessus' *Noriberga illustrata*, 1532.

4. Johannes Turmair, gen. Aventinus, *Sämmtliche Werke*, I (Munich, 1881), 219. Celtis' intervention in behalf of the manumission of a monastic servant in 1504 is the only instance of active social concern, Br. 323, p. 579 and Br. 324, pp. 580f. His sympathies were not with the "common crowd." See chapter VII of *Norimberga*. An insight into the penny-wise Nuremberg burgher mentality is to be gained from Anton Tucher's *Haushaltbuch*, W. Loose, ed. (Tübingen, 1877). Compare Friedrich Roth, *Die Einführung der Reformation in Nürnberg* (Würzberg, 1885), pp. 1ff.

5. Ode II, 12, lines 9-16. See also Br. 50, pp. 81ff.; Br. 82, p. 135. Celtis even discussed with one of his Ingolstadt students his plan of writing a little work entitled *De vera nobilitate*, on the true nobility which stems from the virtue of good deeds, Br. 160, pp. 267ff. Ep. II, 50: De ignavo nobili.

6. The Basel edition of 1495, probably by Johann Bergmann von

Olpe, is identical with Ode III, 10. Compare Campbell Dodgson, "Die illustrierten Ausgaben der Sapphischen Ode des Konrad Celtis an St. Sebald," *Jahrbuch der Kunsthistorischen Sammlungen der allerhöchsten Kaiserhauses*, XXIII (1902), 48ff. Art historians seem to be agreed on Wohlgemut as the probable source of the first woodcut, but are uncertain as to the second. See Br. 91, pp. 149ff.; Br. 114, pp. 190f.; Br. 147, pp. 245ff.; Br., p. 246, note 1.

7. The codex is the famous Clm 14485, Münchener Staatsbibliothek. See also Br. 70, pp. 118f.; Br. 74, pp. 123f.; Br. 75, pp. 125f.; Br. 83, pp. 136ff.

8. Br. 71, pp. 119f.; Br. 73, pp. 122f.; Br. 88, pp. 144ff. Trithemius listed the works of Roswitha individually in both his *Catalogus illustrium virorum*, p. 129, and his Annales Hirsaugienses, p. 126. B. Hartmann, "Konrad Celtis in Nürnberg," *Mitteilungen des Vereins für Geschichte der Stadt Nürnberg*, VIII (1889), 33.

9. Ode II, 26; Br. 80, pp. 132f.; Ode III, 25; Ep. III, 33.

10. Br. 81, pp. 133ff. Cf. Ode III, 22; Am. III, 13, line 34; Ep. III, 34; Am. III, 13.

11. Br. 83, pp. 136, lines 42-49.

## Chapter 5—The Rhenish Sodality

1. Ode III, 5. K. Hartfelder, "Konrad Celtes und der Heidelberger Humanistenkreis," *Historische Zeitschrift*, XLVII (1882), 23ff., describes their relationship, badly misdating the correspondence, however.

2. The most complete monograph on the Rhenish Sodality, G. Bricard, *De Sodalitate Litteraria Rhenana* (Bordeaux, 1893), must be almost completely discounted because of its many palpable errors.

3. Br. 268, pp. 468ff., lists fourteen members, but not all known members. The fact that so many Nurembergers were included suggests that they were included merely because the Roswitha was published in Nuremberg and they were there.

4. Ode III, 24; Br. 279, p. 509.

5. D. F. Strauss, *Ulrich von Hutten* (Leipzig, 1914), pp. 16ff. For Celtis' preoccupation with threesomes, see Ep. II, 63; Ep. III, 22; Am. III, 10, lines 15f. Compare Fr. von Bezold, *Aus Mittelalter und Renaissance*, p. 97.

6. Ep. IV, 59; Ep. IV, 48; Ep. IV, 47; Ep. III, 100.

7. It is extant in Celtis' own miserable handwriting, Nationalbibliothek codex 3748, fols. 236-248ᵛ: Institutio grammatice grece a chunrado protucio celte, Vienne tradita.

8. Am. I, 2.

9. Ode III, 15. See also Br. 237, pp. 396f.; Ep. IV, 60.

10. Ode III, 9; Ode III, 8; Ep. II, 57; Ep. II, 56; Ep. IV, 56; Am. III, 13, lines 39ff.; Am. III, 9, lines 25ff.; Ode I, 1, lines 2ff.

## Chapter 6—The Danubian Sodality

1. "In hoc libello Continentur. . . Impressum Vienne ductu Conradi Celtis Anno M Quingentesimo seculari." The poem to the sodalities was republished as Epod 14 with the Epigrams listing seven sodalities: Septemcastrensis Danubianus, Dantiscanus Vistulanus, Pomeranus Codoneus, Albinus Luneburganus, Alpinus Dravanus, Rhenanus Vangionus et Mosellanus, Necaranus Hercynianus.

2. K. Wotke, "Der Olmützer Bischof Stanislaus Thurzó von Béthlenfalva (1497-1540) und dessen Humanistenkreis," *Zeitschrift des Vereines für die Geschichte Mährens und Schlesiens*, III (1899), 363, errs in holding that the sodality was founded by and named after Christophorus Apitius Meierhof, a member of the third class of Celtis' Poets College.

3. See Br. 175, pp. 287f.; Br. 192, p. 322; Br. 198, pp. 329f.; Br. 199, pp. 331f.; Br. 262, pp. 451f. Compare E. Reicke, ed., *Willibald Pirckheimers Briefwechsel*, I (Munich, 1940), ep. 86, p. 280; J. Schück, *Aldus Manutius und seine Zeitgenossen in Italien und Deutschland* (Berlin, 1862), pp. 63ff.

## Chapter 7—In Maximilian's Vienna

1. Br. 230, pp. 383ff.; Br. 235, pp. 391ff.; Br. 237, pp. 396f. G. Bauch, *Die Reception des Humanismus in Wien*, pp. 87ff., overemphasizes the difficulties between Celtis and the arts faculty. On Celtis' negligence, see Ep. III, 78; Br. 258, pp. 445ff.

2. *Lucij Apulei Platonici et Aristotelici philosophi Epitoma diuinum de mundo Deu Cosmographia ductu Conradi Celtis Impressum Uienne.* It was printed by J. Winterburger in Vienna. Celtis lectured on Apuleius, Ep. IV, 44, 50.

3. On this first edition, presumably done by Winterburger, see E. Klüpfel, *De vita et scriptis*, II, 60ff.; Br., p. 394, n. 1. A second edition with Celtis' name appeared in Vienna in 1515, published by Singrenius and Vietor.

4. P. Joachimsen, "Tacitus im deutschen Humanismus," *Neue Jahrbücher für das klassische Altertum*, XIV, no. 1 (1911), 697ff. Hans Tiedemann, *Tacitus und das Nationalbewusztsein der deutschen Humanisten* (Berlin, 1913), pp. 3ff.

5. It was published presumably by Winterburger around 1500, as were also the *Oeconomia* and the *In hoc libello continentur* in all prob-

ability. L. Forster, *Selections*, p. 13, suggests that Celtis' model for the *Oeconomia* was Martial, book XIV.

6. Ep. IV, 82. Celtis and Greek, Br. 306, pp. 552ff., lines 27f.; Br. 307, pp. 554ff., lines 6ff.; Br. 297, pp. 533f.; Ep. IV, 57; Br., p. 555, n. 1, on Greek books in Celtis' library.

7. Universitätsarchiv MS 14. Matricula Universitatis Vienn. III, 1451-1518, fol. 107ᵛ, col. 1: Udalricus Zwingli de Glaris 4 pf. (Left margin: exclusus); fol. 114ᵛ, col. 1: Udalricus Zwingling de Lichensteig. 29 Pf. (ennig).

## CHAPTER 8—Playwright

1. Ep. IV, 18; Ep. IV, 55. See *Vita*, Br. 339, pp. 609ff., lines 38f.

2. See Alfred Schuetz, "Die Dramen des Konrad Celtis," Vienna dissertation, 1948, an excellent study. In two poems in a small collection published by Peter Bonomus in 1518, *Complurimum eruditorum vatum carmina*, fols. B2ᵛ and C2ᵛ, Celtis recalled the Linz affair and how Grünpeck had served as host. The first edition of the *Ludus* was published May 13, 1501, by H. Höltzel in Nuremberg. The second was included with the *Amores* in 1502.

3. The *Rhapsodia*, published by Johannes Othmar, contained two woodcuts by J. Burgkmair, one of the Bohemian battle, the other of the insignia of the Poets College. On Burgkmair, Ep. V, 62. After many copies of this edition had been published, an additional folio, fol. 24, was added with two more poems by Celtis, to Maximilian and on Apollo. The list of participants in the dramatization is presented in Br., p. 548, n. 1 and pictured in Otto Rommel, ed., *Wiener Renaissance* (Vienna, 1947), opposite p. 240.

4. G. Bauch, *Die Reception des Humanismus in Wien*, pp. 154ff., assembled the materials on this *Ludus*. The woodcut is pictured in Arthur Burkhard, *Hans Burgkmair der Ältere* (Berlin, 1932), table IX. See also Br., p. 576, n. 1.

5. G. Manacorda, "Konrad Celtis' Gedichte in ihren Beziehungen zum Klassizismus und italienischen Humanismus," *Studien zur vergleichenden Literaturgeschichte*, V (1905), 161. On Chelidonius, J. Zeidler, "Das Wiener Schauspiel im Mittelalter," *Geschichte der Stadt Wien*, III, 1, 109ff., 112.

6. The *Melopoiae* of Tritonius expressly stated that the tonation was achieved "ductu Chunradi Celtis." On Tritonius and Celtis at Ingolstadt, R. von Liliencron, "Die Horazischen Metren in deutschen Kompositionen des 16. Jahrhunderts," *Vierteljahrschrift für Musikwissenschaft*, III (1887), 30, n. 1. According to R. Pirker, the model for the first chorus of the *Ludus Dianae* was the qualitative notation of a

hexameter used by Franciscus Niger in the second edition of his grammar, *Grammatica P. Francisci nigri A. veneti sacerdotis oratoris facundissimi*... (Basel, 1500). The second chorus sung in the third act still shows characteristics of the Italian Frottole. It was almost the identical melody as that used by Niger's melody to Horace, Venice, 1480, Carm. I, 30, 13-16. Celtis added the polyphony in both cases, though the actual composition may well have been the work of one of Maximilian's court musicians, though hardly Tritonius, who was in Italy at the time. The polyphony was first species counterpoint. A. Schuetz, "Die Dramen," pp. 147ff., 241, 158f.

7. *Melopoiae Sive Harmoniae Tetracenticae*... *per Petrum Tritonium et alios doctos sodalitatis Litterariae nostrae musicos*... *ductu Chunradi Celtis* (Augsburg: Erhard Oeglin, 1507). This quarto edition was followed by many octavo editions.

8. Ode I, 1, lines 13f.

## CHAPTER 9—Poet

1. Am. II, 9, lines 153f. His books contained the inscription: "Con. Cel. pro. poete sum."

2. Ep. V, 56; Ep. III, 104; Am. IV, 15, lines 1-4; Oraculum Apollonis ad Celtem, *Rhapsodia*, 1505 ed., fol. 13$^v$.

3. Br. 272, pp. 474ff. Br. 273, pp. 484f.

4. Br. 274, pp. 485ff.

5. *Quatuor Libri Amorum Secundum Quatuor Latera Germanie Feliciter Incipiunt* (Nuremberg, 1502). Poems found with the Nuremberg manuscript by Reuchlin and others, but not published, are to be found Br. 276-9, pp. 504ff. Nationalbibliothek Codex 4027, *Fragmenta librorum amorum*, contains a few worksheets prepared by an amanuensis for the publication.

6. Münchener Staatsbibliothek Clm 434.

7. Br. 307, pp. 554ff., line 24. Erwin Panofsky, *Albrecht Dürer*, I (Princeton, 1948), 95, no. 350, no. 412.

8. E. Panofsky, "Conrad Celtes und Kunz von der Rosen: Two Problems in Portrait Identification," *Art Bulletin*, XXIV (1942), 39ff., argues convincingly though not conclusively for the identification of Dürer's companion as Celtis.

9. Br. 280, p. 510.

10. *Libri Odarum quatuor, cum Epodo, et saeculari carmine*... (Strassburg, 1513). F. Pindter, "Die Lyrik des Conrad Celtis," Vienna dissertation, 1930, discusses each ode in detail.

11. The Hartfelder edition of 1881. Trithemius mentioned the *Epi-*

*grams* in his *Catalogus* and *De scriptoribus*. In the preface to the *Amores,* Celtis wrote of his *Centepigrammaton.*

12. Ep. III, 53.

13. Ode III, 17.

14. Br. 343, pp. 619f., line 22.

## CHAPTER 10—Patriot

1. Am. III, 13, lines 51ff.; Ode III, 16; Ep. II, 29-32.

2. *Oratio,* sentences 41-46. Ep. I, 57. Am. I, 15, lines 33ff., 51ff. Ode II, 8; Ep. II, 25. U. Paul, *Studien zur Geschichte des deutschen Nationalbewusztseins im Zeitalter des Humanismus und der Reformation* (Berlin, 1936), pp. 29ff., 42ff. Beatus Rhenanus corrected Celtis for including lands across the Rhine and Danube in ancient Germany, A. Horawitz and K. Hartfelder, *Der Briefwechsel des Beatus Rhenanus,* ep. 423, p. 564.

3. Br. 15, pp. 28f.

4. Br. 267, pp. 461ff., lines 35-54.

5. Br. 267, pp. 461ff., lines 60-69. The literature on the authenticity of the Roswitha dramas resulting from Aschbach's challenge is well known. Edwin Zeydel, "Knowledge of Hrotsvitha's Works Prior to 1500," *Modern Language Notes,* LIX (1944), summarized the research on the problem with some inaccuracies. Zoltán Haraszti, "The Works of Hrosvitha," *More Books,* XX (1945), 87ff., 139ff., in an aggressive and critical argument, maintains that the authenticity is still open to question. F. Merkel and E. Zeydel have promised a further study of the authenticity problem, Research in Progress, no. 6147, *Publications of the Modern Language Association,* LXVII (1952).

6. E. Reicke, ed., *Willibald Pirckheimers Briefwechsel,* ep. 146, p. 485, lines 19ff. After long discussion, including such authorities as Jakob Grimm, it is now generally agreed that the *Ligurinus* is of medieval origin.

7. *Ligurini De Gestis Imp. Caesaris Friderici primi.* Compare Br., p. 598, n. 1; Br. 335, pp. 596ff. On the illustrations in the *Ligurinus* ed. of Oeglin (Augsburg, 1507), see M. Thausing, *Dürer* (Leipzig, 1884), pp. 209ff.

8. *Germania generalis,* II. De situ Germaniae. . . , lines 1-10. Compare Tacitus, *Germania,* chapter 2.

9. *Germania generalis,* II, lines 11-15. See Tacitus, *Germania,* chapter 4. Caesar, too, spoke of their unusual size. Am. I, 14, lines 3ff.; Am. II, 9. Ludwig Sponagel, *Konrad Celtis und das deutsche Nationalbewusztsein* (Bühl-Baden, 1939), pp. 26ff. Ode III, 8, lines 29f.

10. Ode IV, 3, published in the *Epitoma*, 1492, with the last lines mentioning Barbara Cimbrica added later. Ep. V, 52; Ep. III, 1; Ep. I, 50; Br. 216, pp. 359ff. Aeneas had likewise based his accounts of the Lithuanians on travelers' reports, *Europa*, chapter 26.

11. *Norimberga*, chapter 3; Ode III, 28. The Druid idea appealed to Trithemius, Althamer, Aventine, and others. Celtis had the idea prior to the appearance of the *Pseudoberosus* in Rome in 1498.

12. Br. 295, pp. 530f.

## Chapter 11—Philosopher

1. M. Ficino, *Opera*, 2 vols. (Basel, 1576), I, 659. Am. I, 11; Ode I, 29, lines 1ff.; Am. IV, 14, lines 29f.; *Norimberga*, chapter 6.

2. Ep. II, 35. Ode II, 11, lines 45ff. Ep. III, 70-76; Ep. IV, 78; Ep. IV, 66.

3. Ode I, 5. Ode I, 11, lines 69ff.

4. Ode II, 2, lines 77ff.; Ode II, 14; Ep. I, 6: "Ad Jovem optimum maximum."

5. *Vita*, Br. 339, pp. 609ff., lines 132f., "Scripsit Parnasum bicipitem, in quo poetas et theologos concordat." Br. 110, pp. 184ff., may be a reference to this work.

6. Br. 79, pp. 131f., lines 26f. Ep. II, 2; Ep. V, 5; Ep. IV, 17. Ode III, 15, lines 29ff.; Ep. IV, 23; Am. III, 9, lines 47ff.; Br. 2, p. 4, line 43; Ep. I, 6; Ep. I, 19, etc. Ode IV, 9; Br. 3, p. 7, lines 26ff.; Am. IV, 3, lines 60ff.; Ep. V, 40.

7. Ode I, 16. Ode I, 19.

8. Ode I, 5, lines 137ff.; Am. IV, 4, lines 89ff.

9. Br. 275, pp. 494ff., lines 121ff. Br. 101, pp. 165ff., line 22.

10. Ode IV, 6, lines 15-18; Am. III, 12, lines 53-62; Ode III, 15; Am. IV, 3, lines 60ff.; Am. IV, 4, lines 57ff.

11. Ode II, 23, lines 97ff. Ode I, 20; Am. I, 6, line 50; Ep. I, 6, etc.; Epod 13.

12. Epod 12.

# INDEX

# Index

Academia Platonica. See Academy
Academy: of Pomponius Laetus, 15; lack of at Cracow, 17; planned for Ingolstadt, 21; Rhenish Sodality as, 46; "Neacademy" of Aldus Manutius, 60, 61; Poets College as, 68
Ad divam dei genitricem . . . , 32
Ad laudem et commendationem civitatis Bambergae, 36
Aeneas Silvius: crowned with laurel, 6; on Rome, 13; on Nuremberg, 35; depicts Rhine cities, 37; apologist for eroticism, 86; stirs German patriotism, 93–94, 99; on invention of cannon, 95; on Lithuanians, 132n. See also Pius II
Aesticampianus (Johannes Rhagius), 9, 124n
Agricola, Rudolf, 3, 4, 6, 47, 94; promotes neoplatonism, 107; poems to saints, 116
Agrippa of Nettesheim, 102
Aicher, Laurentius, 42
Albert of Mainz, 41
Albertus Magnus, 2
Aldus Manutius, 9, 60, 61, 78
Alexander VI, 96
Alexander Gallus, 5, 54
Alt, Georg, 36
Alt-Oetting, 53, 116
Amerbach, Johannes, 42
Amores, 84–90; Hasilina heroine in, 18; geographic scheme of, 58; and

Longinus' panegyric, 70; Odes compared with, 90; Germania illustrata patterned after, 102; astrology in, 109; concept of Eros in, 114
Antibarbari, 68
Apollo, 65; laurel wreath of, 7; Ode to, 10; muses and, 39; oracle of, 83; woodcuts of, 88, 89. See also Phoebus
Apuleius, 56, 65, 66, 128n
Aquinas, Thomas, 2
Archetypus liberalium artium, 36
Argyrius, Jacobus, 18
Aristides, 36
Aristotle, 50, 106, 107; Brudzewo lectures on, 16; J. Gallus lectures on, 47; Rhenish humanists discuss ethic of, 51
Ars humanitatis, 9, 16, 61
Ars versificandi, 4, 5, 6, 124n; epigram defined in, 91; editions of, 123n
Astrology, 16, 51, 53, 108, 109
Astronomy, 2, 16, 31, 32, 58
Augsburg: members of Danubian Sodality in, 56; Sodalitas litteraria Augustana, 59, 60, 98, 103; Rhapsodia published in, 79; Melopoiae published in, 82; Celtis in Augsburg, 98; Arminius' victory near, 100
Aulularia, 73

Dracontius, Jakob, 47
Dürer, Albrecht, 11, 130n; Sebaldus woodcut by, 41; *Amores* woodcut by, 88, 89; depicts melancholy in *Philosophia*, 109

Eck, Johann, 70, 100
Eitelwolf von Stein, 49
Epicurus, 86
*Epigrams*, 84, 91, 130–131n
*Episodia Sodalitatis litterarie Danubiane*, 56, 57
*Epitoma in utramque Ciceronis rhetoricam*, 24
Erasmus, 5, 39, 45, 62; praises Agricola, 3; *De ratione conscribendi epistolas* by, 24; refuses to write *vitae sanctorum*, 41; letter of Jerome cited by, 68; praises Pirckheimer ladies, 84; transcends local patriotism, 105
Erasmus Australis, 44
Erfurt University, 4, 22
Ermolao Barbaro, 50
Ethics: secular, 31, 32, 33; Aristotelian, 51; moral philosophy, 115–116; virtue versus fortune, 111
*Eunuchus*, 73
Euticus, Heinrich, 20, 58
Eyb, Albrecht von, 36

Fame, 4, 52, 115
*Fasti*, 9, 36
*Fastnachtspiel*, 75, 79
Fate, 109–110
Ferrara, 11, 12
Ficino, Marsiglio, 12, 107, 108, 109, 115
Filelfo, Giovanni Mario, 6
Finck, Heinrich, 80
Firenzuola, Agnolo, 87
Florence, 11, 12, 45
Frederick III, 6–8, 14, 38, 39, 55, 75, 116
Frederick Barbarossa, 98
Frederick the Victorious, 3
Frederick the Wise, 6, 7, 8; woodcut of Celtis and, 89; preface of

Roswitha edition to, 96–97
Freiburg im Breisgau, 43
Fuchsmagen, Johannes, 34, 57, 66, 78
Fusilius, Sigismund, 32, 110

Galfred of Vinosalvo, 5
Gallus, Jodocus, 47
Gelonus, Nicolaus, 50
Geography, 2, 58, 66, 70, 103; Celtis urges study of, 31, 32
George of Saxony, 8
George the Rich, 21
Gerald de Barri, 32
Gerbellius, Nicolas, 52
*Germania*: influence on *Germania illustrata*, 40–41; Celtis' edition of, 66–67; stimulates patriotism, 99–100; etymologies from, 102
*Germania generalis*, 67, 102
*Germania illustrata*, 97, 102; *Norimberga* prelude for, 40–41; Moravia in, 60; *Germania generalis* and, 67
*Germaniae descriptio*, 102
Germany, 32, 35, 41, 50, 52, 62, 65, 84, 97, 103, 109, 113, 116; Celtis to illumine, 19, 40, 102; intellectual reform of, 20, 94; universities in, 23, 27; former glory of, 26, 27; low estate of, 28, 94; new era, 67
Golden age theory, 26, 52, 67, 95, 100, 101
Gossinger, Sigismund, 120
Greek, 12, 27, 86; Celtis' knowledge of, 4, 5, 107, 129n; spoken by ancient Germans, 26, 97, 101, 131n; necessity for study of, 30, 31; Trithemius learns, 43, 48; humanists' knowledge of, 50, 61; promoted at Vienna, 68
Greeks, 7, 48, 76
Grünpeck, Josef, 75
Gutrater, Gabriel (Eubolius), 58

Hartmann von Eppingen, 43
Has, Kunz, 37
Hasilina von Rzytonic, 17–18, 24, 87
Hebrew, 27, 48, 61; Celtis' knowledge of, 4, 50; Tolhopf opposes